Effective Advertising Strategies for Your Business

Effective Advertising Strategies for Your Business

Cong Li

First published in 2014 by
Business Expert Press, LLC
222 East 46th Street, New York, NY 10017
www.businessexpertpress.com

ISBN-13: 978-1-60649-868-2 (paperback)
ISBN-13: 978-1-60649-869-9 (e-book)

Business Expert Press Marketing Strategy Collection

Collection ISSN: 2150-9654 (print)
Collection ISSN: 2150-9662 (electronic)

Cover and interior design by Exeter Premedia Services Private Ltd,
Chennai, India

First edition: 2014

10 9 8 7 6 5 4 3 2 1

Printed in the United States of America.

Abstract

As the media landscape has evolved over the past few years, especially with the emergence of interactive media and social media, the philosophy of advertising is significantly changing. Most businesses realize that the days when they relied on three national networks (ABC, NBC, and CBS) and a few national newspapers to advertise are gone; thus, they begin to find alternatives to standardized advertising. Many of them begin to adopt more individualized advertising approaches, empowered by the Internet technologies.

Although a few high-technology companies—such as Google, Facebook, and Amazon—are showing success in delivering individualized advertising messages to consumers, this approach (including both personalization and customization) is not suitable for all businesses. The problem is that many companies don't know what strategy is the best for their business. The purpose of this book is to describe in detail and discuss the pros and cons of each of the three fundamental strategies of advertising: standardized, targeted, and individualized. The importance of collecting consumer insights and incorporating those insights into advertising messages will be highlighted. No single strategy is absolutely more effective than the others; however, here you are given a real strategy based on a scrutiny of the value proposition of the business and expectations of consumers.

Keywords

advertising strategy, customization, individualization, personalization, standardization, targeting

Contents

Chapter 1   How Does Advertising Function in General?..................1

Chapter 2   What Are the Three Advertising Strategies?...................19

Chapter 3   How Does Standardized Advertising
             Strategy Work? 31

Chapter 4   How Does Targeted Advertising Strategy Work? 43

Chapter 5   How Does Individualized Advertising
             Strategy Work? 55

Chapter 6   How to Gather Consumer Insights for Advertising.......67

Chapter 7   How to Incorporate Consumer Insights
             Into Advertising..79

Chapter 8   How to Integrate Different Advertising
             Strategies Together.......................................91

Notes...101
References 109
Index 121

CHAPTER 1

How Does Advertising Function in General?

This opening chapter broadly describes the philosophies and practices in the advertising world. It also explains several key terminologies widely used in the advertising industry. Specifically, it answers the following questions:

- How is advertising commonly defined?
- How has the Internet changed the advertising business in general?
- Why is advertising a combination of strategic thinking and creative work?
- How should an advertising campaign be executed?
- How should an advertising campaign's effectiveness be measured?

What Exactly Is Advertising?

Traditional Definition

Since this book explains how to select and implement an effective advertising strategy, the first thing that I need to do is to define what advertising is or what, in my opinion, advertising really means. This is not an easy task, at least it is not as easy as it sounds. The truth of the matter is this: Most people encounter hundreds or even thousands of commercial messages per day, and the definition of advertising is largely subject to each person's individual experience. As seen in an article published in the *Journal of Advertising*,[1] numerous definitions of advertising, given by different textbooks, dictionaries, trade organizations, and government agencies exist. It is unbelievably difficult to reach a consensus on what advertising really is, even among those experts who practice or teach advertising for their living.

The major problem of defining advertising is that advertising shares some common characteristics with other forms of marketing communication, such as sales promotion, direct marketing, and public relations. To make a clean and clear distinction between each of these activities is quite challenging. I don't believe that I have the talent to solve this problem, and it is probably unnecessary for me to add to the existing definitions and provide another one. However, it is worthwhile for me to explain how advertising is commonly defined in the field, and put my two cents in as to how it is related to this book.

An interesting question that I frequently get from my students in entry-level advertising courses is: Why are most advertising programs held in the communication school instead of the business school at a university? Intuitively, advertising sounds very business-oriented, doesn't it? Well, yes, advertising is certainly a part of business operations. However, more importantly, in essence it is a type of communication. A classic way to describe communication is: Who says what in which channel to whom with what effect?[2] If you think about this description, advertising indeed is communication. Most existing definitions of advertising actually reflect this nature and capture some or all of the following five elements: (1) create a paid message; (2) reach more than one person; (3) include an identified sponsor; (4) use mass media; and (5) persuade.[3] In other words, advertising can be regarded as a paid communication process from an identified sponsor, using mass media to persuade or influence many people. Such a definition worked well for advertising practices before the Internet arrived. For example, a company pays for a television commercial on a national network and the advertising message gets delivered to many consumers who watch TV and who presumably will buy the product or service advertised. The Internet, however, is a game changer. Over the past two decades, the Internet has significantly changed how companies and consumers send and receive messages. As a result, the fundamental philosophy of how advertising works or should work has been altered.

New Meanings

If we further examine the five aforementioned elements that are typically attached to advertising, we can argue that at least three of them are not applicable anymore. First, media used to be categorized into two camps based on their functions: interpersonal media and mass media. The purpose of interpersonal media is to facilitate one-to-one communication. Examples of these media include telephones and letters. In contrast, mass media make one-to-many communication possible by sending messages to the mass. Conventional mass media, of course, refer to newspapers, magazines, radio, and television.

The Internet blurs the line between interpersonal media and mass media. Within an Internet environment, not only is one-to-one communication possible, but also there are one-to-many, many-to-one, and many-to-many.[4] Therefore, the Internet is a mixture of interpersonal media and mass media. From an advertising perspective, this feature is critical because it upends the basic logic of advertising which is that advertising messages should be paid and that they need to go through mass media and reach more than one person. The new understanding today is: (1) advertising may not be paid, (2) advertising may not go through mass media, and (3) advertising may not necessarily reach more than one person at one time.

A primary reason why communication scholars classify media into either interpersonal media or mass media is because mass media are subject to the so-called gatekeepers, while interpersonal media are not. For example, when you make a phone call or write a letter to another person, you are in full control of the message flow. There is no middle man in between you and the other party. That is not the case with mass media because ordinary people don't have access to it. Consider a conventional mass medium, such as television. It is the gatekeepers, such as journalists, reporters, and editors who decide which messages get sent to the masses. If you want to have a voice there, you need to pay and your message is subject to scrutiny. Unfortunately, the price is high, especially when you are referring to some mass media with a national impact. I guess you know how expensive Super Bowl ads are. Yes, $4 million for 30 seconds![5] It's crazy, but true. It's a small wonder that most businesses cannot afford this type of luxury ads, but the good news is that the Internet provides every company opportunities to advertise for free or with little expense.

Social media such as Facebook and Twitter are excellent examples to illustrate the point that the Internet has significantly changed the advertising world. When you set up your business account on Twitter, for instance, you are empowered to communicate with consumers in many different ways such as one-to-one (replying to an individual follower's tweet) and one-to-many (posting a tweet for all followers). The beauty of this is: You are in control of the message exchange and you don't pay big bucks to the media to do this for you. Thus, whatever messages you create on the Internet become advertising, no matter whether they go through your corporate website, social media account, or other platforms.

The purpose of my writing this book is not to teach you how to build an effective corporate website or on what social media platform you should set up a business account. Instead, I want to focus on the third change the Internet brings to advertising practices that I mentioned earlier: Advertising may not necessarily reach more than one person at one time. Traditionally, a common method for pricing an ad is based on how many people it is expected to reach. The more, the better. Now we know why Super Bowl ads are so expensive. Yes, over 100 million people are expected to watch the game![6] If you do the math, you will find out that you pay approximately four cents for each person potentially exposed to your ad, given that it costs you $4 million in total. It doesn't look that expensive now, right? This is why many companies are eager to seek media vehicles that can help them reach as many people as possible and they are willing to pay for these media channels. Another reason is that many people believe advertising expense is a good indicator of marketing effort: The more money spent on advertising, the greater the effort—meaning that the company really has faith in the product so as to advertise it heavily.[7]

You don't have $4 million to spend on advertising? Okay, don't worry. The emergence of new media presents alternative ways to advertise. Instead of trying to reach a gigantic number of people with one shot, you can communicate with each individual consumer at one time. This type of communication is often termed as personalization or individualization.[8] Such an idea of communicating with each individual consumer is not really new, but it is the Internet that makes such communications inexpensive and affordable. Many times these individualized communications are even more effective than advertising to the mass. One thing to note, however, is that I am not suggesting that individualized communication is always superior to other types of communication. In fact, in certain cases, it is not the ideal approach. In later chapters, I will lay out the fundamentals of three major advertising strategies and discuss when each of them is suitable for a business and should be adopted: (1) standardized, or talking to many consumers; (2) targeted, or talking to a group of consumers; and (3) individualized, or talking to each individual consumer. I will also elaborate on how advertising messages should be created based on each strategy and how to measure their effectiveness.

Two Sides of Advertising

Being Strategic

Advertising has two sides: strategy and creativity. Some people mistakenly think advertising is all about making things visually appealing and entertaining—this certainly is a misperception. Advertising does involve a great deal of creative work and certain software usage, but knowing how to use Photoshop or InDesign doesn't necessarily mean that you are doing advertising in a correct way. An effective advertising campaign must be both strategic and creative.

From an operational standpoint, a typical full service advertising agency has four departments that perform different jobs: account management, account planning, creative development and production, and media planning and buying. Apparently, developing creative work is one function of an agency, among many. Specifically, people in the creative department, such as art directors and copywriters, are responsible for developing creative messages in a certain strategic direction. This direction is usually generated from consumer research conducted by account planners who work in the account planning department. Thus, developing ad messages is in fact a collaborative process between strategy and creativity.

The history of incorporating both sides (strategy and creativity) in advertising goes back to the 1960s. In the old days, strategy didn't play a critical role in the advertising world. Many advertising campaigns were developed and implemented without knowing much who the target audiences were and what they wanted. The concept of account planning that advertising messages need to reflect consumer insights was originated in the UK by two advertising agencies (JWT and BMP) in the late 1960s.[9] In 1981, this idea was introduced to the United States and made its debut at an agency in New York (Chiat\Day).[10] Today, it has been widely recognized and adopted in advertising communities across the world.[11]

In its formative years in the UK, account planning was considered as a response to the need to understand changing consumer cultures.[12] The most critical function of account planning, therefore, is to apply knowledge and understanding of consumers to the development of advertising messages.[13] When Apple was ready to promote its Macintosh, it asked its advertising agency to focus on the computer's power. However, through consumer research, the agency learned that consumers actually wanted radical ease of use. Accordingly, the advertising campaign switched the focus to emphasize that anyone could operate the system. As predicted, the campaign turned out to be very successful and Apple computers became popular.[14] This example illustrates why it is necessary and important for advertisers to understand consumers.

The term *account planning* may seem somewhat ambiguous and odd to many people, including advertising professionals, but in general, people agree that account planning is mainly about strategy or research.[15] Account planners are generally regarded as the researchers in an advertising agency because they are involved in all sorts of research activity such as collecting market information, analyzing and interpreting consumer data, conducting personal interviews, and moderating focus groups.[16] In advertising practitioners' own words, "a hugely important part of planning is to understand how people feel" and "to make ads that strike a chord with people."[17]

More importantly, account planners are considered to be strategists and insight miners, meaning that they need to develop a well-grounded and justifiable strategy based upon their research findings.[18] The final tangible output of this strategy formation process is a single-page writing called *creative brief*. It summarizes all key issues discovered in consumer research and pinpoints a strategic direction that will foster creative ideas and solutions.[19]

Although advertising cannot live without either side, strategy and creativity don't always work well together. They often tend to be adversaries rather than cooperative teams.[20] The truth is that in most cases the creative side of advertising is more visible than the strategic side. This is probably why many people underestimate the importance of strategy to advertising. Although account planners are continuously involved in the whole advertising campaign process, the exact contribution of their consumer research and strategic thinking to the effectiveness of ad messages is difficult to be assessed with finality.[21] In reality, people use different measures to evaluate the job of an account planner such as the client's feedback, the number of award-winning, and the extent of media coverage of the advertising.[22] None of these measures seems to be universally acceptable.

Being Creative

Creativity may be one of the most complex human behaviors to describe and explain.[23] There is no magic formula to turn an uncreative person into someone full of creative ideas, but research has shown that creativity may be related to risk taking. In the advertising world, it is believed that people who are more willing to take risks tend to be more creative.[24] Thus, I tell my advertising students to try something different each day, a special food or a unique dress or something else, if they want to pursue their careers in an advertising agency via the creative route.

Creativity in advertising is always associated with terms such as *creative thinking*, *problem solving*, *imagination*, and *innovation*. Different from other forms of creativity, advertising creativity must achieve a specific business objective. If the business objective is not fulfilled, the creative endeavor will be considered failed.[25] As mentioned earlier, the creative work in advertising needs to be guided by a strategic direction. Therefore, advertising creativity possesses two significant features. The fundamental characteristic is divergence—the ad message must contain elements that are novel and unusual in some way.[26] At the same time, the message must also be appropriate and relevant—it must be meaningful and valuable to the audiences such as showing the product being used in circumstances familiar to them.[27] In other words, the message needs to reflect a correct understanding of advertising strategy and target audiences.[28]

In the literature, the importance of creativity to advertising effectiveness is generally acknowledged and accepted, although there are multiple ways to define and measure advertising creativity.[29] Some people like to use the opinions from advertising professionals to judge whether a certain ad is creative or not. Others prefer to make decisions based on whether the advertising campaign wins a creative award. For example, in a study that tested the effects of advertising creativity,[30] ads from award-winning campaigns and ads from random network television programs were selected to represent high and low creativity, respectively. It was shown that highly creative ads were deemed as more interesting, more memorable, and also more likeable. In another study that examined the relationship between advertising creativity and ad likeability, consumers were asked to name their most liked and disliked television commercials.[31] Separately, those commercials were rated by an expert panel on the level of creativity. As the study results suggested, a larger proportion of liked commercials were considered to be highly creative than disliked ones.

Although creative ads may generate greater attention and lead to more favorable effects, such conclusions need to be interpreted with caution because most research studies of advertising creativity are conducted in a forced-exposure setting: research participants are explicitly told to process some stimulus advertising message. In more realistic settings, of course, people have a choice of whether to engage or not engage with the message. More creative ads may not necessarily trigger deeper mental processing than less creative ones.[32] Moreover, the creative approach doesn't work universally with all product categories or age groups.[33] Older consumers may prefer less creativity than younger consumers. Also, creativity may be inappropriate for medical or health-related products.

Finally, it needs to be pointed out that a person's judgment of creativity is quite subjective. For instance, advertising professionals and consumers often hold different opinions with this regard. For advertising practitioners, creativity tends to be what makes their client's business objective reachable, whereas for the public, creativity tends to mean whether the advertising message is relevant to their needs. In a study that tested whether advertising practitioner views of advertising creativity were different from those of consumers, a group of advertising agency people and a group of television-viewing consumers were surveyed and interviewed.[34] The study results revealed significant differences between the two groups in terms of how they evaluated the creativity of certain television commercials. In another study, it was shown that people are more interested in the brand information and tend to perceive it to be of higher quality when exposed to more creative advertising messages in comparison to less creative ones.[35] However, such effects are determined by individuals' perceived creativity. At the end of the day, consumers' perceptions are what matter most.

To Educate or to Entertain?

Being Informative

What is the ultimate goal for companies to advertise? As reflected in common advertising definitions described earlier in this chapter, it is to persuade and influence consumers. Companies need to select a specific approach to execute the campaign because advertising can be executed in various ways that lead to different persuasion effects. In general, there are two execution options: One that is designed to appeal to the rationality of consumers by using objective information describing a product's attributes or benefits, and the other that is designed to appeal to consumers' emotions by using drama, music, and other emotion-eliciting tactics.[36] A typical way to label these two approaches is rational versus emotional, although other terms also have been used in the advertising and marketing literature (informational versus transformational; factual versus evaluative; thinking versus feeling; hard sell versus soft sell).[37]

Discussions exist on how these two execution approaches work. The central focus is under what circumstances one approach is superior to the other. The explanation of using the rational approach mainly comes from information processing theories in social psychology. According to this perspective, consumers are rational decision makers who actively search for, attend to, and evaluate data to make brand choices.[38] In this case, advertising serves as one of the primary information sources for them to make purchase decisions.[39] Thus, informational advertising aims to change consumers' beliefs of the advertised brand by presenting strong arguments about product attributes.[40]

A well-established theory in social psychology, the Elaboration Likelihood Model (ELM),[41] for example, states that people take different routes (central or peripheral) to process information. When they are highly involved with something, they tend to process a message related to that subject carefully. In other words, they will process the content deeply if the message appears to be relevant to them. Their attitudes are likely to change, in this case, if the arguments presented in the message are strong and evidence-based. This is why informational advertising should be used for thinking products (high involvement products) such as cars, furniture, or cameras.[42]

As argued by many academics and practitioners, whether to adopt the rational or emotional approach depends on several factors such as what type of product is promoted in the advertising message and via what media channel the message is delivered.[43] It even depends on in what country the product is advertised.[44] Print media, for example, are more suitable for the rational approach because print is reader-paced and allows more message detail and explanation.[45]

Being Entertaining

Different from the rational approach, the emotional approach is grounded in the feeling side of consumption instead of the thinking side. The goal of this approach is to connect consumers to the advertised brand by creating an emotion such as humor, love, fear, and guilt.[46] Apparently, these emotions can be either positive or negative.[47] Emotional appeals have been used in many advertising campaigns, such as in Pepsi-Cola's ("Get that Pepsi feeling") and Burlington's ("Never go to bed with a sheet you don't love").[48]

The most frequently used emotional appeal in the advertising world is humor. The effects of using humor in advertising have been widely tested in academic and industrial research. Humor helps attract people's attention and enhance liking of the ad and the advertised brand.[49] However, it doesn't appear to offer an advantage at increasing the message's credibility and persuasive effects. Thus, it is important to keep in mind that an ad being entertaining is not equal to it being effective, although we see funny ads all the time.

First of all, the audience factor will influence responses to humor. What is funny to a certain gender, ethnic, or age group may not necessarily be funny to others. For example, research has shown that men tend to enjoy sexual jokes more than women.[50] Moreover, the use of humor is more appropriate for advertising consumer nondurables such as soft drinks, alcohol products, snacks, and candy,[51] but it is not suitable for high involvement products because people tend to have strong relationships with these products. Making fun of such relationships may be considered as threatening.[52] Finally, humorous ads are more proper for broadcast media than print media because television viewers and radio listeners are passive message receivers and they are generally waiting to be entertained.[53]

Being Informative and Entertaining

Is it possible or wise to adopt both the rational and emotional approach and include multiple appeals in a single advertising message? Well, yes, sometimes. It depends to whom the advertising message is sent. Strong persuasion effects tend to occur when the appeal used in the message matches the message receiver's preference for processing information.[54]

There exist some measures in social psychology that gauge a person's tendency to engage in and enjoy thinking (e.g., the Need for Cognition scale).[55] People who score high on such measures are believed to be active information seekers. The rational approach, thus, is more effective for these people.[56] Similarly, there are measures that have been used in the field to evaluate to what extent a person responds to an emotional appeal (e.g., the Need for Emotion scale).[57] People who score high on such scales are believed to be emotion seekers and they consistently experience their emotions with greater strength when exposed to emotionally provocative stimuli.[58] In a study that tested the effects of emotional versus non-emotional appeals,[59] it was shown that emotion seekers were more receptive to emotional advertising.

An interesting thing is that some people may be comfortable with both information processing styles (rational versus emotional) and they switch back and forth whenever necessary. These people are generally considered as combination processors.[60] To advertise to them, both rational and emotional appeals can be included in the advertising message.

Obviously, to make these judgmental calls on whether to adopt the rational approach, or the emotional approach, or both, you need a good consumer database in hand so that you know whom you are talking to in your advertising. Therefore, it is critical to know how to use existing consumer databases and also how to set up new databases for the purpose of making strategic decisions.

Memory, Attitude, and Behavior

Do Consumers Remember You?

No matter what strategy or execution approach is adopted in an advertising campaign, it is always important to measure its effectiveness. However, it still remains a mystery today with regard to how exactly advertising works and how advertising effects should be measured. A fundamental debate exists between two schools of thought.[61] On the one hand, many business managers believe that advertising is effective only when it sells. Thus, data of sales, profit, and market share are the only valid measures to determine whether advertising is working or not. On the other hand, some academics and advertising practitioners have proposed hierarchy-of-effects models to explain how advertising functions, suggesting that there is a series of stage between the point of unawareness of a brand or product and the ultimate purchase or sale. These types of models have been in the advertising and marketing literature for more than 100 years, in one form or another.[62] According to these models, there are other measures rather than mere sales to evaluate advertising effectiveness such as brand awareness, brand feature awareness, brand preference, and intention to buy.[63]

Taking an often cited article in the *Journal of Marketing* for example,[64] it argues that a person will go through seven steps from being a potential buyer to becoming a real buyer: (1) unawareness of the existence of the brand or product; (2) mere awareness of the brand or product's existence; (3) knowledge of what the brand or product has to offer; (4) a favorable attitude toward the brand or product; (5) preference of the brand or product over all other possibilities; (6) a desire to buy the brand or product and the belief that the purchase would be wise; and (7) an actual purchase of the brand or product. Advertising helps facilitate this hierarchical process by serving as a primary information source.

There is no concrete conclusion on the debate between these two camps of measurement proposition (the sales-focused perspective versus the hierarchy-of-effects perspective), but most people agree that both of them have flaws. First, the sales figure should not be used as the sole indicator of advertising effectiveness because sales are subject to the influence of many non-advertising factors such as competitive actions, economic conditions, government regulations, and so on.[65] Moreover, advertising effects are usually delayed.[66] Employing advertising today doesn't guarantee an immediate increase of sales tomorrow (it may take effects months later or even years later). Finally, the exact contribution of advertising to sales cannot be easily separated from that of other related marketing communication activities such as public relations and promotions.

Similarly, the hierarchy-of-effects perspective is not without problems. It is unlikely that people always experience certain steps before they buy something, although occasionally it does happen. Put simply, hierarchy-of-effect models cannot explain the psychology of people's impulse shopping behavior. To remedy this shortcoming, scholars have provided alternative explanations of these models and argue that the order of each step may not necessarily be fixed. That is to say, it is perfectly plausible that a person buys a brand or product or likes a brand or product before he or she gains knowledge of its attributes and benefits.

Built on this long-lasting measurement debate, the current mainstream understanding is that advertising effectiveness should be measured from three different aspects without any particular order: cognition (such as attention to brand information, memory of brand messages, and learning of brand attributes); affect (such as attitude toward the ad, attitude toward the brand, and preference of the brand among alternatives); and behavior (intention to purchase, word of mouth, and actual purchase).[67] Thus, if you have implemented an advertising campaign, you need to examine its effects in these three ways. Favorable results from either one of these areas may suggest that the campaign is successful.

First of all, you want to know whether people have paid enough attention to your ad and remembered its content. A common method to measure attention and memory in the advertising world is to use message recall and recognition, meaning that you ask people what they can recall or recognize from the ad. In general, recall is more difficult to achieve and considered to be a higher level of memory because it tends to be an open-ended question without any hint (e.g., "What brand did you remember seeing in the ad?"). In contrast, recognition is more like a multiple-choice or true-or-false question (e.g., "Among the following five brands, which one did you remember seeing in the ad?" or "Do you remember seeing the following brand in the ad, yes or no?"). It needs to be pointed out that recognition may be associated with more measurement errors because people have a chance to guess in responding to a recognition question. To control such errors at a reasonable level, a good tactic is to include false alarm items in the question. For example, in a consumer survey regarding Super Bowl commercials in the year 2006,[68] people who watched the game were randomly selected and asked to identify whether they had seen certain brands' commercials. Eight false alarm brands that didn't advertise during the game were included in the questions. As the survey results showed, approximately 27 percent of respondents mistakenly thought they had seen either one or more of those false alarm brands during the Super Bowl broadcast. Of course, in this case, their data need to be handled carefully and interpreted with caution.

Memory of advertising messages can also be measured with sophisticated physiological tools such as eye tracking devices. This is certainly a newer and fancier way to do consumer research. The idea is to introduce natural science measures to social science research. However, this type of research can only be conducted in a laboratory environment and may not be very realistic. When people are asked to wear an eye-tracking device and read a magazine in a laboratory, for example, they probably will get nervous and behave very differently from the way they would normally do at home.

Do Consumers Like You?

Next, you need to measure consumers' attitudes. People often form their preferences on the basis of affective elements such as liking, feelings, and emotions. Two types of affective responses are typically used in the advertising industry: attitude toward the ad (e.g., "How much do you like the ad?") and attitude toward the brand (e.g., "How much do you like the brand advertised in the ad?)."[69] These types of measure are often based on a numerical scale such as a 1-to-5 or 1-to-7 point continuum. It is worth noting that attitude formation may be a long-term process rather than a one-time shot, especially the attitude toward the brand. Three to four times of message repetition are probably necessary before consumers' attitudes can be reasonably stabilized.

What is the relationship between a favorable attitude toward the ad or brand and an actual purchase? It is for sure that these two things are not perfectly connected to each other. The fact that people like your brand or your advertising doesn't necessarily mean that they will buy your products. However, some research in the literature did show a significant correlation between attitude and purchase, although the relationship is not that strong.[70] The bottom line is this: Fostering a favorable attitude is likely to bring long-term values and benefits to your business rather than short-term benefits (this is the fundamental doctrine of public relations). Just look at the crisis that Target recently experienced regarding the incident of credit card breach,[71] and you can imagine how many consumers it might potentially lose due to the public's growing negative attitude toward the brand.

Do Consumers Act as You Wish?

Finally, consumers' behavior needs to be measured. In the strictest sense, only actual purchases or sales can be defined as real behavior. However, such a definition may be too narrow to be helpful. The Internet today in fact presents many non-purchase behavioral metrics that businesses can use. For example, in an Internet marketing course that I teach, I ask each of my student teams to set up an account in Google AdWords and they have $200 to run a campaign for a local client. One of the criteria used to judge the students' performance is the total number of clicks that they generate from their campaign. When people click an ad on a website or a mobile device, it means that they are somewhat interested in the content. Although a click doesn't necessarily lead to a purchase on the fly, it is certainly a promising and valid behavioral measure. Another example, when you use social media such as Facebook or Twitter to communicate with consumers, many consumer actions may help your business even though they are not real purchases per se. These actions include that consumer like your Facebook posts, mark your tweets as their favorite, and so on.

I will use a real scenario from the industry, Effie Awards, to close the discussion of advertising effectiveness measures. Effie Awards are well-recognized symbols of effective marketing communication campaigns across the world. Judges of these awards are asked to evaluate a campaign's effectiveness based on its strategic planning, creative idea, and real business outcomes.[72] Therefore, the judgmental decision is really a combination of several different perspectives. In conclusion, to use sales as the only criterion for advertising effectiveness is not only unfair, but also misleading. A good advertising campaign should be strategically guided, and its effects need be assessed from multiple angles including cognition, affect, and behavior.

Chapter Summary

The key takeaways of this chapter are summarized as follows:

- Today's advertising practices are significantly different from those of the old days, due to the influence of the Internet. Specifically, advertising nowadays may not be paid, may not go through mass media, and may not necessarily reach more than one consumer at one time.
- Strategy and creativity are two inseparable sides of advertising. Therefore, developing effective advertising messages is a collaborative process between strategic thinking and creative work.
- Rational and emotional are two typical approaches to execute an advertising campaign. They are grounded in the thinking side and the feeling side of consumption, respectively. To adopt which approach depends on the type of advertised

product or service, media used for advertising, and audiences of the advertising campaign.

- The effectiveness of an advertising campaign should not be judged based on sales only. Instead, it needs to be measured from multiple aspects including cognition, affect, and behavior.

CHAPTER 2

What Are the Three Advertising Strategies?

This chapter provides a general description of three different types of advertising strategies: standardized, targeted, and individualized. Specifically, it answers the following questions:

- What is the standardized strategy, and what does standardized advertising really mean?
- Why can standardized advertising be effective?
- What is the targeted strategy, and what does targeted advertising really mean?
- Why can targeted advertising be effective?
- What is the individualized strategy, and what does individualized advertising really mean?
- Why can individualized advertising be effective?

Standardized Strategy

Who Are You Talking to?

As I mentioned in Chapter 1, advertising strategies can be broadly categorized into three types: standardized, targeted, and individualized. In this chapter, I explain the conceptual differences of these three types of strategies in detail. It is worth pointing out that the term strategy can be applied to many business processes such as manufacturing products, determining product prices, selecting distribution channels, and promoting products. What I am about to elaborate here is how a company should pick an appropriate strategy for its advertising, primarily from a communication perspective, although this strategy may be closely or remotely related to the company's entire business orientation, such as marketing, finance, information system, research and development, and operations. It should further be noted that the order of these three types of strategies is not based on a superiority ranking. It would be incorrect to say one strategy is superior or inferior to another. All three types of strategies are widely used in today's business world. From a chronological perspective, the standardized strategy has dominated advertising or marketing practices for a long time until some companies started to try the targeted strategy in the 1950s. During the past decade, the individualized strategy has gradually gained popularity, largely due to the rapid growth of a few high-technology giants such as Google, Facebook, and Amazon.

Among the three types of strategies, standardization is probably the default of many companies. The fundamental idea of the standardized strategy is to neglect the market heterogeneity and treat all consumers in the same way. Its underlying logic is that consumers are similar to each other and have common needs and wants to a large degree. Therefore, it is unnecessary to differentiate them and create some artificial distinctions. A nice example to illustrate people's common needs is salt, a product they use daily on their dining table.[1] People need salt and cannot live without it. However, no matter what specific branded salt people buy, the product is essentially the same to everyone.

The major benefits of standardized strategy are to save business cost, avoid consumer confusion, and improve efficiency. Regarding advertising, the standardized strategy can be considered as a one-to-all communication because the company is attempting to talk to all consumers.[2] Apparently, by producing and sending the same message to all consumers, the company leverages the economies of scale. Coca-Cola's famous "Coke is it" campaign of the 1980s helps illustrate this notion very well. If you search the keyword "Coke is it" on YouTube, you will find a bunch of television commercial videos there. Literally, what's depicted in those commercials is that all people (including different gender, age, ethnicity, and occupation) want to drink coke in all contexts and settings (including dancing, singing, kissing, playing, exercising, and even arguing and fighting). The ads certainly suggest that drinking coke is the "most refreshing way to make the most of everyday, wherever you go and whatever you do."

Coca-Cola has stopped using the standardized strategy to promote Coke today because the product has lost its universal appeal due to the increasing health-related concerns among consumers. Based on the market demand, Coca-Cola has developed alternative products for people (such as Diet Coke, Coke Zero, and Coke Zero Caffeine-Free), who like soft drinks but are worried about taking in too many calories or too much caffeine. Coca-Cola's decision to produce and promote different products to different consumer groups is a smart move. However, it would be premature to conclude that it is always wise to do so and regard standardization as an old-fashioned strategy. Believe it or not, most companies today are still doing standardized communication, and they are doing it every day. For example, a company's corporate website is one of the major communication channels for consumers to get to know this company. How many companies present different information to different consumers on their websites? Well, very few (such as Google and Amazon). In most cases, when consumers log into a company's corporate website, they are exposed to the same set of information, which means that the company has standardized its online communication. Another interesting point is that, even if a company has the capability to present different information to different consumers, it may not always be a good idea to do so because it can be controversial. For instance, Orbitz (www.orbitz.com), a website for planning and booking travel, has found that people who use Mac computers spend as much as 30 percent more per night on hotels, so the company starts to show Mac users more pricy hotel options than PC users.[3] Sounds unfair, doesn't it? I cannot predict whether Orbitz will lose some consumers due to this controversial strategy, but I use Mac, and I am not particularly happy about being treated differently when booking my travel online.

Why Do You Think They Want to Listen?

In the case of standardized advertising, consumers are passive participants in the communication process. The advertising message typically features a general product that appeals to all consumers, and the company selects some universal media that reach many viewers to send the messages out. It needs to be noted that standardized advertising means that a company sends the same message to all consumers at one time, but it doesn't mean that the company should use the same advertising message over and over again (the company's brand name, logo, and slogan should be kept consistent across different ads, though). The general consensus in the advertising world is that an advertising message needs to be repeated three to five times to achieve the optimal results, but after those repetitions consumers' interest in the ad will wear out quickly.

A classic scenario when a company needs to determine whether to standardize its advertising or not is that its businesses expand from one nation to another. Hundreds of articles have been published in advertising, marketing, management, or business journals, debating on whether companies should adopt the standardized strategy when they move to other markets.[4] It is widely believed that if consumer demands across nations are similar, the standardized strategy will be an ideal choice. In a study that surveyed American and Japanese multinational companies' subsidiaries operating in five European countries (United Kingdom, France, Germany, Italy, and Netherlands), it was shown that standardized advertising indeed enhanced the companies' financial performance due to the similarity of consumer culture in those countries.[5]

Although consumers' preferences change from time to time and differ from person to person, it is reasonable to argue that what people essentially want and search for are high-quality products at optimally low prices.[6] In a famous article published in the *Harvard Business Review* over 30 years ago, a former professor at the Harvard Business School, Theodore Levitt, proposed that companies should focus on innovation and developing better-quality products instead of differentiating consumer groups based on their shopping differences. The driving force of this proposition is the rapid development of Internet technologies. Different from the brick-and-mortar context, the Internet environment has significantly decreased consumers' search cost for specific products or services.[7] Using the Internet to compare alternative products and services on price and other attributes has become a natural and easy task for many people.[8] Thus, eventually what matters most to the success of a company is whether its product or service is of high quality and whether it is priced lower compared to the competitors.

The truth is: people nowadays rely heavily on the Internet to search for product and service information for their decision making, and they trust the information they find online. For instance, a few years ago I conducted an experiment, testing the effects of electronic word-of-mouth.[9] Guess what? I am a college professor, so I am interested in knowing how word-of-mouth on the Internet will affect my teaching (students do talk about their professors on the Internet!). My coauthor and I collected the data from a popular professor-rating website RateMyProfessors (blog.ratemy-professors.com), and we found that those online ratings did affect actual course enrollment. Our data analysis results suggested that professors who received positive word-of-mouth on the RateMyProfessors website tended to have more students enrolled in their classes than those who didn't. I guess students are always looking for good quality professors (who teach interesting and useful content and who also grade fairly), and they use new media to gather relevant information to make their decisions. Thus, the general conclusion is: If you have a good quality product at a lower price, the standardized strategy may be an appropriate choice for you.

Targeted Strategy

Who Are You Talking to?

The idea of the targeted strategy is in fact built on that of standardized strategy. The primary motivation for companies to use such a strategy is to differentiate their products or services from the competitors and gain a fair market share. The underlying logic of targeted strategy is that a certain product or service may be suitable or appropriate for some consumers only (instead of for all consumers). For instance, a refrigerator with no storage compartment for frozen foods is suited for home freezer owners whose frozen-food storage needs have already been met.[10] Companies that wish to use the targeted strategy should be able to identify whom the most suitable consumers are and what social group (such a group is commonly termed a market segment) they belong to. The objective of targeted advertising, then, is to communicate with consumers in that group. In essence, targeted advertising is one-to-n communication.[11]

Since the targeted strategy involves a process of cutting the whole marketplace into several segments, it is also called market segmentation.

The strategy of dividing markets into segments started in the mid-1950s,[12] reflecting many companies' desire to view a heterogeneous market as a number of smaller homogeneous markets based on different product preferences among different consumer groups.[13]

What specific segment a company should focus on is largely a judgment call. Theoretically speaking, the selection of a target consumer group should be based on its potential to bring profits to the business. In practice, a company may adopt the targeted strategy based on unique needs of any consumer group. This consumer group can be either strictly defined, or loosely defined. An important assumption here is that people in the same target group share common characteristics or interests. Companies can divide the marketplace up by combining certain consumer characteristics, such as yuppies or buppies, or selecting a subculture, such as Latinos or gays and lesbians.[14] It should be noted that some of these targeting methods are based on common sense while others require more in-depth consumer research. For example, it is common sense that dating websites target people who are not married—of course a specific dating website can further target a more specific consumer group such as Hispanic singles or Christian singles. However, as seen in another example,[15] the target group of Audi A3 is young males (aged between 24 and 30) who earn a high annual income (more than $150,000). The selection of this specific consumer group is certainly beyond common sense, and it needs to be based on consumer research data.

Why Do You Think They Want to Listen?

Because targeted advertising assumes that people in the target group share some common characteristics and interests, companies should draw on knowledge of their selected target group to create advertising that carries a specific meaning for consumers in the group (this can be regarded as an encoding process).[16] When the message gets to consumers through specific media, they will be involved in a decoding process. People in the target group are more likely to correctly interpret the meanings that the company intends to deliver than people outside the group due to their knowledge and experience as members in that group.[17] In the advertising literature, the most researched targeting method probably is ethnic targeting, meaning that companies cut the whole marketplace into several segments based on consumers' ethnicities (such as non-Hispanic Whites, Hispanics, African Americans, Asian Americans, and so forth).

Unfortunately, there is always a chance that a person who receives a targeted message will not be aware that he or she has been targeted with the communication.[18] The effect of targeted advertising is largely dependent on how strongly consumers in the target group identify with that group membership. For example, in a study that tested the effects of print ads with different models among African American females,[19] it was found that those who were strongly connected to the African American ethnic identity evaluated the ads that featured black models in dominant positions and that were placed in an ethnic medium (such as *Essence* magazine) more favorably, whereas those who were weakly connected to the African American ethnic identity were more positive toward the ads that featured white models in dominant positions and that were placed in a general-audience medium (such as *Glamour* magazine). Moreover, how a person interprets a targeted message is also subject to his or her individual experience. For instance, an African American consumer may attribute a company's salute to Black History Month as a sign of respect for the African American community if he or she believes that the company has shown support for the group in the past.[20]

It is important to note that an individual belongs to multiple consumer groups, depending on how the market is segmented. Using myself as an example, I am an Asian (I share the same ethnicity with other Asians) and I have a doctoral degree in mass communication (I share the same educational background with other people who have a doctoral degree). I am also a member of a badminton club at my university (I share the same hobby with other badminton players). I can continue this list and describe myself from various angles until you get the whole picture, but that won't be necessary. The simple conclusion here is that a person's identity is a combination of many different group identities. Thus, a message can be targeted for a consumer based on any of his or her group memberships (this is why some people may argue that targeted communication may essentially be the same to individualized communication). When the consumer is strongly identified with a specific group membership, a targeted message incorporating that feature is likely to be persuasive to him or her.

It is also important to note that some of a person's group identities may be passively assigned to (something that he or she is born with such as gender and race), but others may be actively chosen (something that he or she pursues such as a sports club or a hobby). Generally speaking, a consumer's identification with a group that he or she actively joins tends to be emotionally stronger. Such a group can be formal or informal, and can be organized in a face-to-face manner or in a computer-mediated environment. For example, in a study that discussed the function of brand community,[21] it was shown that people who drive Saab cars love to form a community based on their common Saab spirit. They like to call themselves Saabers. To show their recognition and respect of this distinctive group identity, they will beep or flash the lights when they pass someone else driving a Saab on the road.

Individualized Strategy

Who Are You Talking to?

The idea of the individualized strategy is not a new invention. It has been known and discussed by different terms (such as profiling, filtering, tailoring, customization, personalization, and one-to-one marketing) for many years.[22] The general goal of individualized communication is to offer the right message to the right person at the right time to achieve specific persuasion effects.[23]

Think of the following scenario: You are the owner of a small restaurant and you have a loyal customer who comes in every weekend. You know him or her so well that you not only can call him or her by name but also you know what his or her favorite dishes are. Once he or she comes in, you will greet him or her by name. You remember where he or she likes to sit and what he or she likes to order. Thus, you can accommodate him or her preciously based on his or her preferences without even asking him or her.

In the above example, you incorporate a specific consumer's characteristics (such as his or her name) and preferences (such as his or her favorite dishes) when communicating with him or her. This is exactly how the individualized strategy should work. Such a strategy represents an extreme form of market segmentation, with a target segment of size one.[24] It can be considered as a one-to-one communication. The primary reason why some companies adopt the individualized strategy is because they consider the market to be so fragmented that each individual consumer needs to be treated in a unique way. For example, consumers tend to have different tastes of music, thus it is a wise idea to individualize music products to them.[25] Pandora (www.pandora.com), the leading Internet radio service, is well known for its individualized music playlists. To recommend new but relevant music to each individual consumer is at the heart of the Pandora business. As Pandora's Chief Scientist, Eric Bieschke, said, the company has "spent the last thirteen years working on the most sophisticated music recommendation system ever created."[26] In another example, Viacom is currently planning to launch a new interactive children's TV channel "My Nickelodeon Junior" based on the market demand of individualized TV programs. As described in a recent news report on the *Wall Street Journal*,[27] people used to watch a TV channel with programming scheduled by a network or sift through on-demand services to find a show they prefer, but now they have the third choice—to create an individualized channel for their kids. The parents will be able to individualize the content that airs on My Nickelodeon Junior by indicating their preferences for seven themes such as word play and super-sonic science. According to these preferences, the channel will choose specific content to air from hundreds of episodes in its database.

Such ideas of individualized music playlists or TV channels sound pretty fun and cool, right? You may wonder why they were not implemented much earlier. Well, in the past, to individualize something was not only costly, but it was also inconvenient. For instance, to purchase a standardized suit at a shopping mall is much quicker and generally cheaper than to get an individualized suit from a tailor. It is the rise of the Internet that has made the individualized strategy more economic, and also necessary nowadays. Applications of personalized search, recommendations, price, and promotions are good examples to illustrate that today's business environment is ready for personalization.[28] Compared to before, consumers today are more empowered and they are the center of communication. In general, people want to be active participants in product development, purchase and consumption process, and as the co-producer of service offering.[29] Therefore, companies need to create individualized messages for consumers when they expect such individualization.

Why Do You Think They Want to Listen?

The common practice of individualization in the advertising world is to create different messages for each consumer based on his or her demographics (such as gender, age, education background, and so forth) or past behavior (such as past purchases). It seems reasonable to assume that people with different demographic characteristics or behavioral histories will respond differently to messages.[30]

The major benefits of individualized communication are threefold: (1) the time and effort needed for consumers to make decisions can be significantly reduced; (2) the message can help consumers find products or services that better match their preferences; and (3) consumers may enjoy the feeling that they discover some new products or services that they are not aware of before.[31] Also, individualization may be a sign of benevolence—it shows that the company wants to treat each consumer with respect and the company is concerned about his or her welfare.[32]

The effects of individualized communication have been widely tested in many different disciplines such as marketing, communication, public health, psychology, and information science. In an interesting psychological experiment,[33] for example, research participants were asked to weigh, measure, and mix several chemical substances in a laboratory. There were plastic gloves and face masks on a table along with other materials and equipment for people to use. Of course those chemical substances were harmless (they were actually water, cooking oil, and powdered soap combined with food coloring), but there was a warning sign suggesting them to use mask and gloves for the safety reason. The purpose of the study was to test whether people would comply with the warning. Two types of warning signs were tested, one being standardized ("CAUTION! IRRITANT. Use Mask and Gloves") and the other being personalized (replacing "CAUTION" with each participant's first name). The study findings showed that a personalized warning sign had greater alerting effects as a higher percentage of people exposed to the personalized sign wore mask and gloves.

However, I have to point out that although many studies have been conducted in the past few years to test the effectiveness of individualized messages, the study findings in the literature are somewhat mixed or even contradictory. It is important to keep in mind that individualized messages are not always more effective than standardized or targeted messages. For instance, in two studies that centered on the same topic (to examine how individualization might improve web survey response rates), the research findings were very different. In one study,[34] a non-individualized e-mail (it said "Dear student" in the salutation) was sent to 1,000 students and an individualized e-mail (it incorporated the message recipient's name in the salutation such as "Dear John Smith") was sent to another 1,000 students, both inviting them for an online survey. The study results showed that the response rate generated by the individualized e-mail (57.7 percent) was higher than that generated by the non-individualized e-mail (49.1 percent), and such a difference was statistically significant. However, in another similar study where the effects of non-individualized e-mails (with an impersonal salutation such as "Dear student" and an impersonal e-mail address of the message sender such as surveyresearch@institution.edu) and individualized e-mails (with a personal salutation such as "Dear Jane" and a personal e-mail address of the message sender such as "jsmith@institution.edu") were compared, no significant difference was discovered regarding the response rates.[35]

It is also important to point out that consumers don't always process advertising messages consciously. Oftentimes, they process information at a subconscious level.[36] Still remember the Elaboration Likelihood Model from Chapter 1?[37] Yes, people will process a message deeply only when they are motivated to do so. That is to say, different advertising strategies may end up with the same effects if people don't realize what strategy the company is using (this is known as random communication effects). In the following chapters, I will further explain when and how a company should adopt an appropriate advertising strategy and minimize random communication effects.

Chapter Summary

The key takeaways of this chapter are summarized as follows:

- The fundamental idea of the standardized strategy is to neglect the market heterogeneity and treat all consumers in the same way. Thus, standardized advertising essentially is a one-to-all communication. All consumers receive the same advertising message.

- A standardized advertising message may be effective if it promotes a high-quality product with an optimally low price that all consumers want.
- The fundamental idea of the targeted strategy is to view a heterogeneous market as a number of smaller homogeneous markets based on different product preferences among various consumer groups. Thus, targeted advertising essentially is a one-to-n communication. Consumers in the same target group receive the same advertising message.
- A targeted advertising message may be effective if it features a group membership that consumers in that group feel strongly connected to.
- The fundamental idea of the individualized strategy is to consider the market as extremely fragmented and each individual consumer needs to be treated in a unique way. Thus, individualized advertising essentially is a one-to-one communication. Each consumer receives a different advertising message.
- An individualized advertising message may be effective if it incorporates a unique feature of a specific consumer such as his or her past shopping behavior.

CHAPTER 3

How Does Standardized Advertising Strategy Work?

This chapter provides a detailed description of the standardized advertising strategy and further explains when this strategy should be adopted and how it should be implemented. Specifically, it answers the following questions:

- What core business value a company should have if the standardized advertising strategy is adopted?
- What expectation the consumers should have from the company if the standardized advertising strategy is adopted?
- What consumer insights should be generated from research to implement the standardized advertising strategy?
- How should a standardized advertising message be created?

When Is Standardized Strategy Needed?

Proposition of Your Business Value

If you are a business manager, what advertising strategy should you adopt? I recommend that you conduct a two-step analysis before you make the decision: (1) evaluating your core business value and (2) evaluating your consumers' general expectation.

First of all, you need to figure out what true value your business brings to the consumers. Such a business value proposition will be based on not only your own business, but also your competitors. You need to determine what stands out to be the unique value that differentiates your business from others. If this value has a universal appeal to all consumers, the standardized strategy may be appropriate to adopt. Of course, the term all doesn't mean all in a literal sense. In this context it stands for many or most. No company is capable of persuading all the people to become its customers. Even if there were such a magical company, it would soon be destroyed because it would be such an extreme monopoly!

Many companies do provide universal values that attract consumers. These universal values include many different things such as health, family, entertainment, love, friendship, and so forth. For example, suppose that you are the owner of a fitness center. Based on a careful examination of your center and major competitors in the same area, you find out that your center's unique value is that it opens 24 hours a day and seven days a week (and no competitor operates in this way). This suggests that you may be able to use the standardized strategy because operating 24/7 is a convenience feature that suits every consumer's workout schedule no matter what specific operation hours he or she prefers. It makes more sense to promote this value in your advertising in a standardized way (such as telling all consumers that they can come to the center for exercise at any time they prefer) rather than in a somewhat targeted or individualized way (such as telling different consumers that they can come to the center for exercise at different times). Let's use another example, if you manage a barbershop and you truly believe that the barbers working at your shop can do hairdressing for any consumer, it probably would be a good idea to standardize your advertising to acquire customers. The true value that you want to promote in the advertising message would be the barbers' skills in doing all sorts of hairstyle cuts.

I want to point out, though, that this business value proposition needs to be reasonably objective and be based on concrete evidence or common understanding. For instance, if you want to claim that the average price of your products or services is lower than that of the competitors', it needs to be the case. This low price value should be easily recognized by consumers and readily accepted by them as well. Wal-Mart is a good example to illustrate this point because it is well known for offering consumers low prices. A few years ago, Wal-Mart discovered that a simple commonality shared by many shoppers is that they look for deals (but they don't necessarily want cheap products), thus the company decided to change its motto from "Always low prices. Always." to "Save money. Live better." to attract more consumers.[1] If you think about this slogan, it certainly has a universal appeal. Who doesn't want to save money, and who doesn't want to live better?

Once you have defined the true value of your business, you probably want to stick with it for at least a while in your advertising. One of the main advantages of standardized strategy is to help you build up a consistent brand image.[2] You surely don't want some consumers to perceive your brand as a certain type of business while others consider it to be something else. The whole point of integrated marketing communications in the business world today is in fact along this line: to create a consistent brand image across different media channels and with various marketing efforts.

Expectation of Your Consumers

To understand consumers' expectation is as important as it is to evaluate your business' core value. On the one hand, you need to ensure that your business value has a universal appeal to all or most consumers. On the other hand, you need to make sure that consumers don't expect much more than that universal appeal. In other words, if you decide to adopt the standardized strategy, the assumption is that you believe consumers don't expect to be treated differently from each other. Too much variety in the communication between the company and the consumers would be unnecessary, unfair, and even absurd. A good example to demonstrate this argument is what consumers would generally expect when they pull into a gas station.[3] In this case, the consumer's job is fairly simple: to fill up the gas tank of his or her car. The choices he or she faces are usually limited: 87-octane, 89-octane, and 93-octane. Thus, it is unlikely that the consumer would expect much targeted or individualized communication in this scenario. If you were the owner of the gas station, it would be unnecessary for you to communicate with each consumer in a unique and different way. How much difference does it make if you tell a specific consumer that you have reserved some fresh 89-octane for his car? Not much, indeed.

Moreover, sometimes consumers may not want to be remembered or targeted by the company. They would prefer to be considered as a general member of the public instead of a special consumer. This happens quite often when consumers have specific predetermined goals in their mind and they don't want to be distracted by anything else. For instance, when a person goes to a bank to deposit a check (but nothing else), he or she may not want to be treated in a special way based on his or her income level. The simple way would be to communicate with him or her with standardized information. However, if the bank attempts to measure his or her demographic features and behavioral preferences, either in an explicit or implicit way, and then sends somewhat targeted or individual- ized mortgage information to the person (either right away or later), it is likely to be considered as irrelevant and intrusive.

However, when consumers expect a great variety of information from the company, the standardized strategy may not be suitable anymore. For example, if you were a real estate agent, your clients probably would expect you to treat them in very different ways. To send individualized housing information to a prospective buyer based on his or her unique needs will be much more effective than to send standardized information to him or her. Put simply, sending information of properties priced above a million dollars to consumers whose maximum purchasing power is half a million dollars will not only waste their time, but also your own time. It will ruin your reputation as well.

How to Craft a Standardized Message

Consumer Insights

Since the basic assumption of standardized strategy is that consumers share similar needs and wants, you don't have to set up a database at each consumer's individual level as long as you know (or you can predict) what consumers prefer in common. That is to say, it is unnecessary to associ- ate a particular characteristic with a specific group of people or a specific individual. Instead, you want to find out a common appeal that most people will be attracted to. From this perspective, the requirement of data accuracy for the standardized strategy is much lower than that for the targeted strategy or individualized strategy.

Although a database containing each individual consumer's features and characteristics is not needed for you to implement the standardized strategy, consumer research and market research are still critical and key consumer insights cannot be neglected in the advertising message production process. Both secondary research and primary research can be used to generate these insights. The main purpose of these research activities is to detect something cool and trendy that a large variety of consumers would appreciate and like. The secondary research, in this case, primarily involves following the most recent and hottest cultural and sports events, both online and offline. The primary research, on the other hand, means that you go to the field and talk to people and figure out what is cool and what is trendy in their eyes for the time being. Using a direct quote of an advertising professional who is responsible for analyzing new trends, his job is "to go from Tucson to Los Angeles to Vegas to Pittsburgh and live in student unions vicariously, spend time in retail settings and then tap into academia."[4]

For a long time, the advertising industry is believed to be a perfect venue to reflect, and even create, fads and trends.[5] Advertising campaigns play an extremely important role in the production of popular culture in the United States.[6] It is pretty common to see famous musicians, artists, and sports stars in advertising messages to promote specific brands or products (such as the basketball superstar LeBron James and the comedian Kevin Hart's appearance in a Samsung commercial). As a matter of fact, many companies do wish to become a part of the popular culture. For instance, McDonald's once hired an agency to encourage hip-hop musicians to incorporate the Big Mac into their songs. Each time the song is played on the radio, the musician gets paid.[7] In another example, Microsoft teamed up with the hip-pop performer Jay-Z in a campaign called "Decode Jay-Z with Bing" in 2010.[8] The objective of the campaign was to promote Microsoft's search engine Bing and Jay-Z's new autobiography "Decoded" at the same time, in a much unexpected and cool way. For one month, reproduction of entire pages of "Decoded" appeared in locales mentioned in those pages, including many surprising outlets such as the bottom of a hotel swimming pool, the lining of a jacket, and the felt of a pool table. Clues about those page locations were given on Bing, as well as by Jay-Z's Facebook and Twitter accounts. People could follow the pages on Bing and assemble the book online. Everyone who located a page was also automatically entered into a contest for a grand prize.

The campaign led to terrific results: Bing saw an 11.7 percent increase in visits and "Decoded" hit the best-seller list for 19 straight weeks.[9]

As reflected in the previous examples, to use shared cultural icons is a common practice for the standardized strategy. These cultural icons typically enjoy a great deal of popularity among a large variety of people across different gender, age, marital status, occupation, and so forth. The key is to create a connection between the advertising message and each message recipient and show something that all people would care.

In addition to discovering what cool cultural icons can be included in a standardized advertising message, another important function of consumer research and market research is to suggest what media vehicles are the most appropriate for such a message. For the standardized strategy, you certainly want to select media channels that can impact lots of people regardless of their different demographic features. In other words, such a channel should be a neutral medium via which advertising messages get delivered and received. The Super Bowl broadcast is an excellent example of such media vehicles, although it is too expensive for small businesses to buy. For instance, the 2014 Super Bowl aired on Fox turned out to the most-watched U.S. television event of all-time with 111.5 million viewers.[10] The household rating and share for the game were 46.4 and 69.0, respectively. The 46.4 rating means 46.4 percent of American households that own at least a TV set tuned in to watch the game, while the 69.0 share means that 69 percent of American households that own at least a TV set and have their TV set on during the game time tuned in to watch it! On top of these amazing figures, there were 5.5 million unique visits to Fox Sports online, and there were 25.3 million tweets from pregame to postgame.[11] Based on these data, it seems very reasonable to conclude that everybody watched the 2014 Super Bowl game and talked about it, no matter whether he or she was a die-hard football fan.

Another great example of using media to reach everybody is to advertise on the Times Square billboards. It costs between $1.1 million and $4 million a year to do so, which is the most expensive format of outdoor advertising in the entire world.[12] The logic of such pricy advertising is that thousands of pedestrians and drivers pass by the Times Square area every day and they will be exposed to the messages on the billboards. Moreover, those billboards make tons of incidental appearances on TV shows, especially every New Year's Eve when millions of people tune in to see the ball drop.[13] Thus, no matter whether people physically go to the Times Square for travel or other purposes, there is a chance that they will see the advertising messages on those billboards on TV.

If your company doesn't have a big budget to advertise during a Super Bowl match or on one of the Times Square billboards, that is perfectly fine. There are many other less expensive media options waiting for you. No matter what specific broadcast, radio, newspaper, magazine, website, or other outlet you eventually choose to do your advertising, the media vehicle needs to be somewhat general. Do not pick a magazine or a radio program that clearly focuses on one certain consumer group only, for example, to deliver your standardized advertising messages. Those media vehicles are more suitable for targeted messages, instead.

Message Creation

To implement the advertising strategy that you have selected for your business, whether it is standardized, targeted, or individualized, you should think of an effective way to incorporate the key consumer insights in creating the advertising message. This is always a challenge, even for very experienced advertising professionals. The same information can be framed in very different ways and lead to different persuasion effects. A classic example is 50 percent off versus buy one get one free.[14] The same celebrity can also endorse the same brand or product from very different perspectives. You, as a business manager, probably won't get into the process of writing specific copies or creating certain graphics for an ad, but you do need to participate in determining how the information should be presented in the ad.

Given that standardized advertising is a one-to-all communication, the advertising message should contain something that appeals to the general public. The most common methods adopted by companies for standardized advertising included using humor (making the ad funny), sexual appeals (making the ad sexy), and social responsibility (making the ad ethical). As a matter of fact, you probably get to see all these types of ad every day. The simple reason of using these appeals in advertising is that most people want to be funny, sexy, and ethical.

As mentioned in Chapter 1, humor is a universal appeal that has been widely used in advertising campaigns. For example, Wonderful Pistachios' debut Super Bowl commercial featured the South Korean rapper Psy in a Gangnam Style.[15] The ad shows a standardized strategy since the company believes that this funny dance has a universal appeal to the public in the United States (the Gangnam Style music video has almost 2 billion views on YouTube as of February 2014). In fact, the Gangnam Style dance has been performed by everyone from President Obama to Google executive chairman Eric Schmidt.[16]

Besides humor, sexual appeals also have been frequently used in advertising, no matter whether it is for promoting something related to sex or not.[17] Sexual content in an ad can be verbal (such as sexual innuendo) or visual (such as partial nudity and suggestive posture).[18] Moreover, it can be depicted in either an explicit (such as that the advertising copy directly suggests the use of a certain fragrance results in a sexual outcome) or implicit way (such as that an attractive model posts next to an automobile).[19] The prevalence of sexual content in advertising has been repeatedly discussed in academic research and industry reports. As seen in a study that analyzed ads in six consumer magazines in 1993,[20] 53 percent of heterosexual couples were featured in an engagement of explicit sexual contact (such as passionate kissing or simulated intercourse) in the sample ads. A later study that analyzed ads in the same six magazines in 2003 revealed a similar pattern of how sexual appeals were used in advertising.[21] For example, female models were sexually attired about half the time in the sampled ads.

Sexual appeals are widely used in advertising, simply because many companies believe sex sells.[22] This adage may be true. For example, GoDaddy, a domain name registrar and web hosting provider, is well known for its sexy campaigns (remember its 2013 Super Bowl commercial where the supermodel Bar Refaeli gave a lengthy kiss to a nerd?). When it aired its first Super Bowl commercial in 2005, GoDaddy was a $100 million company but it grew to a $1.3 billion company eight years later.[23] It is apparent that the company's core business value has nothing to do with sex, but sexual appeals are used to promote its brand image because registering domain names and hosting websites are general services that may potentially be used by everybody.

According to a review of sex-in-advertising effects studies,[24] using sexual appeals in advertising can generate favorable persuasion effects although the research findings reported in those studies are not entirely consistent. Most studies are based on some experimental designs where the effects of ads with different levels of sexual imagery are compared. For instance, ads with images of female models in varying degrees of revealing clothing (low, medium, and high) are compared to each other as well as to a control ad (such as an ad with the product only but with no model). The general conclusion seems to be that sexual information in an ad tends to attract the viewers' attention and be subsequently remembered. A sexual ad is also believed to be more engaging, involving, and interesting than a nonsexual ad. The use of sex in adverting may also lead to the viewers' stronger physiological reactions (measured in electrodermal response).[25] However, since sexual content in an ad tends to attract the viewers' attention and processing resources, it is possible that they will have few resources available to process other information in the ad, especially when the sexual appeal is not closely relevant to the product or service being promoted.[26] Thus, it may be better to use sexual appeals for certain products or services (such as fragrances, designer clothing and accessories, health and beauty products, tobacco, and alcoholic beverages) but not others (such as financial services, medicine, and computers).[27]

In addition to humor and sex, another universal appeal commonly used in advertising is corporate social responsibility. A company's advertising campaign that focuses on its affiliation with nonprofit organizations or support for a good cause is typically termed corporate advertising or institutional advertising.[28] The objective of such advertising is to build a good reputation for the company, given that the general public is increasing concerned with many social and environmental issues (such as global climate change, transportation safety, rights of minorities, and so forth). To produce this type of goodwill advertising, a number of activities can be featured in the advertising message, including corporate philanthropy (such as giving to charities), the company's environmental record (such as establishing pro-environment policies), and workforce diversity (such as balancing the percentage of women and minorities on the board).[29]

These corporate social responsibility efforts generally can lead to favorable effects, as seen in a review of research studies in this area.[30]

The public tends to respond positively to a company when it promotes a good cause. For example, LG implemented an advertising campaign "Give it a ponder" in 2009 to encourage teenagers to text more responsibly.[31] The idea of this campaign is based on the fact that mobile bullying is affecting millions of teens and tweens (41 percent of them admit that they have sent, received, or forwarded a text message with rumors about someone that are false) as more of them get cell phones with web access. To help teach teenagers to think before texting, LG created several online videos in a humorous tone, showing kids grew ponder beards before texting. The campaign received heavy media coverage and turned out to be effective. It was shown that 69 percent of teens who saw the campaign videos said the ads made them more careful about texting.

In another campaign "Cultivate a better world" designed by Chipotle a couple of years ago, the company attempted to educate the public about where their food came from.[32] The objective was to connect people to a sustainable food movement. Of course, Chipotle was a part of the movement. Specifically, the company set up a foundation dedicated to creating a sustainable and healthy food future. It also reinvented its loyalty program to reward people for learning about the issues related to food production, and held a one-day free food and music festival in Chicago. Finally, the company created an educational short film called "Back to the start," focusing on complex issues in the fast food industry such as animal confinement, environmental pollution, and chemical usage. The results were quite amazing: the film was viewed more than 8 million times online and the campaign surely earned lots of free media coverage as well.

Chapter Summary

The key takeaways of this chapter are summarized as follows:

- To adopt the standardized advertising strategy, you need to ensure that your business' core value has a universal appeal to all consumers.
- To adopt the standardized advertising strategy, you also need to ensure that your consumers do not expect to be treated differently from each other in the communication process. In

other words, they prefer to be treated as a general member of the public rather than a special consumer.

- To implement the standardized advertising strategy, you do not need to set up a database containing each individual consumer's features and characteristics. However, you do need to conduct research to find out something cool and trendy that a large variety of people will appreciate and like. Your standardized advertising is supposed to reflect these fads and trends.

- You should select neutral media channels for your standardized advertising because they can reach lots of consumers regardless of different demographic features.

- The standardized advertising messages that you create must contain something that appeals to the general public. The most commonly used appeals include humor, sexual appeals, and social responsibility.

CHAPTER 4

How Does Targeted Advertising Strategy Work?

This chapter provides a detailed description of the targeted advertising strategy and further explains when this strategy should be adopted and how it should be implemented. Specifically, it answers the following questions:

- What core business value a company should have if the targeted advertising strategy is adopted?
- What expectation the consumers should have from the company if the targeted advertising strategy is adopted?
- What consumer insights should be generated from research to implement the targeted advertising strategy?
- How should a targeted advertising message be created?

When Is Targeted Strategy Needed?

Proposition of Your Business Value

Similar to what you must do before adopting the standardized strategy, you need to evaluate your core business value and consumers' general expectation before you decide to use the targeted strategy. The essence of the targeted strategy is to deliver a message to a group of consumers based on their common characteristics or preferences.[1] It is assumed that people in this group will respond to the message differently from the general public because they share some unique demographics, values, lifestyles, or behavioral tendencies.

To adopt the targeted advertising strategy, your product or service should have a clear and distinctive appeal to a particular group of consumers. People in this group should easily recognize that what you are promoting in the advertising message is not a standardized product or service, but something particularly relevant to them. It needs to be noted that the unique business value that you focus on in the message can be either functional (such as that your product or service can only be used by people in a certain group due to their unique skills or features) or emotional (such as that your product or service is wanted by people in a certain group due to their desired social status or so).

The main challenge of this targeted process lies in how you identify the target consumer group. It is basically a process of market segmentation. There exist multiple ways to segment the marketplace, such as demographic segmentation, geographic segmentation, psychographic segmentation, behavioral segmentation, and so forth.[2] The most frequently used approach is demographic segmentation, meaning that you choose to promote your product or service to consumers of certain gender, age, ethnicity, educational background, income level, or a combination of those demographic variables. This is probably the easiest way to do market segmentation too, because demographic variables, such as gender, age, and ethnicity, are easy to recognize and measure. Besides demographic segmentation, geographic segmentation is also widely used in advertising practices, which means that depending on where consumers live—urban, rural, suburban, North, South, and so forth—you divide them into groups and assume that people in different groups will respond to your advertising messages differently.

However, in some cases, people in the same demographic group or living in the same geographic area do not necessarily show consistent preferences or attitudes. Thus, you may need to use more sophisticated methods such as psychographic segmentation to figure out what particular consumers your business really attracts. The idea is to categorize consumers into various groups based on research of how they spend money, their patterns of work and leisure, their interests, opinions, and self-evaluations.[3] These psychological variables, apparently, are more difficult to measure than demographic and geographic variables. You need to collect such information via well-defined survey questionnaires. For example, to find out whether people value stability over risk and prefer to live a conventional life, you may ask them to rate their agreement on a scale (typically from 1 to 5, representing from "strongly disagree" to "strongly agree") with statements such as "I do not like to take risks" and "I live a conventional life."[4] Based on the data that people provide in the survey, you then use some advanced statistical methods such as hierarchical clustering to classify them into various groups. The objective of such a statistical treatment is to partition the survey respondents into somewhat homogeneous groups with respect to their attitudes, beliefs, values, or interests while at the same time maximizing the differences between each group.[5] For example, VALS™ is a system created by the research firm SRI International, aiming to test the psychological factors that drive different patterns of consumer behavior. Depending on how people respond to a survey,[6] they can be classified into eight groups including innovators, thinkers, believers, achievers, strivers, experiencers, makers, and survivors. According to Strategic Business Insights (the former Business Intelligence division of SRI International), people in different groups enjoy different lifestyles and prefer different brands.[7] For instance, thinkers' favorite car brand is Subaru, whereas achievers' favorite is Honda. Strivers prefer coke classic, while innovators prefer sparkling water.

In addition to psychological questions, you may also ask people questions about their particular behavior and do segmentation accordingly. This is often called behavioral segmentation. Taking an early study in this area for example, 415 VCR owners were surveyed and categorized into five groups based on their frequency of recording TV programs and viewing rented or purchased prerecorded tapes: time shifters, source shifters, videophiles, low users, and regular users.[8] People in different groups were found to differ in their motives to buy a VCR. In a similar study that was conducted more recently,[9] people were categorized into six groups based on their reported frequency of 14 online activities in a survey (such as purchasing goods, downloading music, searching for jobs, playing games, trading stocks, participating in chat forums, and so forth): web generalists, downloaders, self-improvers, entertainment seekers, traders, and socializers.

Another example of segmentation can be found in a well-cited communication theory—Diffusion of Innovations.[10] This theory discusses how and why new ideas and new technologies spread out in the society. Depending on varying degrees of readiness to accept new ideas, practices, and objects, people can be categorized into five groups: innovators (about 2.5 percent of the population, representing the first individuals who adopt an innovation), early adopters (about 13.5 percent of the population, representing the second fastest group of people who adopt an innovation), early majority (about 34 percent of the population, representing people who adopt an innovation faster than the average member of the society but not as quickly as innovators and early adopters), late majority (about 34 percent of the population, representing those who adopt an innovation after the average member of the society), and laggards (about 16 percent of the population, representing the last group to adopt an innovation).

It is really up to you to decide how to do market segmentation and what consumer group to target for your business. In some cases, this decision may be arbitrary. Essentially, you want people in the target group to associate themselves and their peers with your product or service. Advertising can certainly help set up this association, although it may take a long time. I will use one of my research studies to explain the function of advertising in this aspect. In that study, my coauthors and I examined the effects of brand ethnicity, and we found that Hispanic consumers tended to consider some brands to be Hispanic but others to be American although those brands might carry similar utilitarian values.[11] The reason of this phenomenon is that people interpret the meaning of a brand (i.e., product or service) based on their past experiences. Such experiences are usually long-term oriented and affected by advertising and other factors. For example, in the study we discovered that many Hispanic consumers regarded Navarro to be a Hispanic brand because of its Hispanic origin and its targeted advertising toward Hispanic communities. One research participant from Venezuela specifically said, "I received their advertising flyers in my mailbox all the time … and I think everyone who works in Navarro speaks Spanish but not everyone speaks English." Old Spice was also considered to be a Hispanic brand although it did not originate in Latin America. We asked people why they associated Old Spice with Hispanics, and one of our focus group participants said, "Every Latino guy I know used Old Spice. It reminded me of my dad, my uncle. It's just such a classic scent for many Latino men."

Expectation of Your Consumers

Compared to the standardized strategy, the targeted strategy essentially creates more options for consumers. In other words, consumers would expect some variation of message or choice in a targeted communication process (not as little variation as in a standardized communication process), but not too much (not as much variation as in an individualized communication process). The fundamental logic of this strategy is that people want a certain number of choices to fulfill their unique needs, but giving them too many choices would be unnecessary and inefficient. For example, while an automobile manufacturer may be able to offer 20 million possible variations of a sports car, most consumers feel comfortable choosing among 20 or so models at a local dealer.[12] Thus, creating millions of different advertising message to promote all possible variations for each individual consumer doesn't sound like a wise idea. It may be more efficient just to promote different car models based on their features and target specific consumer segments. The company can do geographic segmentation, for instance, by emphasizing the car's safety in cities where vehicular deaths tend to happen frequently, while emphasizing the car's reliability in cities where the rate of auto accidents is lower than the national average.

No matter what segmentation method you end up using for your business, you need to make sure that people in the target group do share some important characteristics and they are aware of it. Moreover, they should recognize that your advertising messages are somewhat related to the characteristics. It means that the message you deliver to the target consumers will be relevant to their group and help them enhance their group identity. This group identity should be a crucial part of how those people define themselves.

To make your brand (or communication) more relevant to the target group, sometimes you can invite people in that group to give feedback. For example, Texas Instruments once designed a calculator (TI-92) that specifically targeted school teachers. To ensure that the calculator fully addressed the needs of this target group, the company invited thousands of school teachers to offer feedback. The calculator's design specification was finalized after several rounds of such company–consumer interactions.[13]

To make targeted communication more effective, you also need to understand via what media channels consumers in the target group expect to receive targeted messages. For instance, most companies that are active in Hispanic marketing believe that Spanish-language broadcast is more effective in reaching Hispanics than Spanish-language newspapers.[14] Of course this judgment is based on research of how Hispanics habitually use mass media.

Finally, I have to point out that targeted communication is not always more effective than standardized communication. There is a chance that you may not be able to accurately predict how consumers react to your targeted advertising.[15] When people don't want to associate themselves with a certain group (even though they are a member of that group) or they think the message is irrelevant to the group, the effects of targeted communication can be negative.

How to Craft a Targeted Message

Consumer Insights

Similar to the standardized strategy, the targeted strategy does not require a database at each consumer's individual level. However, consumer research and market research are extremely important for you to craft an effective targeted message. Without solid research data, it is almost impossible to come up with a message that will be relevant to the target group. Both secondary research and primary research will be helpful in determining what common characteristics consumers in the target group share (these are the key consumer insights) and how to incorporate that information in creating advertising messages.

First, you can use secondary research data to figure out what particular consumer group your business may want to target. Typically, you pay a third-party market research firm to gain access to those data. I will use MRI+ database[16] as an example to illustrate how secondary research can help you define the target consumer group. When I log into the database, I look through the category of travel in the most recent report and search for those consumers who are more or less likely to take a cruise. I will use the traditional demographic segmentation or geographic segmentation in this case. For instance, when I look at the age variable, I find out that people aged between 55 and 64 are more likely (about 23 percent more likely) than the general public to take a cruise. However, people aged between 18 and 24 are much less likely (about 29 percent less likely) to do so. Therefore, it seems to be a good idea for a cruise line to target senior citizens rather than college-age individuals. Moreover, when I look at the location variable, it shows that people who reside in the South are more likely (about 17 percent more likely) than the general public to take a cruise, but people from the Midwest are less likely (about 27 percent less likely) to do so. Thus, a cruise line can also use location as a key variable to define target consumers, by focusing on the South instead the Midwest. I am using age and location as examples here, but the database certainly offers more information. I can continue searching for differences across gender, ethnicity, educational background, marital status, occupation, annual household income, and others. Based on those differences, I then determine who the ideal target consumers are.

Secondary research can give you a good sense of how consumers differ from each other, primarily from a demographic and geographic perspective. However, to discover the most significant and important characteristics that people in the target group have in common (i.e., the key consumer insights that you want to incorporate in your advertising messages), you should conduct primary research such as interviews, focus groups, and surveys.

I will use two brands in the diaper industry, Pampers and Luvs, as examples to show how primary consumer research can help facilitate the process of targeted advertising. In the case of Pampers, the company was trying to target Hispanic expectant mothers and music was used as a key to make the connection between the brand and the consumers.[17] Based on the consumer research, Pampers found that music was the most powerful cultural force for Hispanics, and Hispanic moms typically considered music as a crucial element in educating their kids. Thus, Pampers produced a very innovative event, the "Bellies Concert," one that was for babies in the womb. The concert took place at the New World Center in Miami. Specially designed belly phones that enabled the babies to enjoy music played (orchestrated Latino lullabies) were provided to those new moms who attended the concert. In the end, this advertising campaign helped Pampers gain a higher level of brand awareness among Hispanic new moms. The fans on the Pampers Latino Facebook page also doubled.[18]

In the case of Luvs, this small diaper brand with less than 10 percent market share found a unique way to compete with bigger players in the industry. To make the brand distinctive, the company decided to exclusively target a unique group of consumers: second-time moms.[19] Through primary consumer research, Luvs found some common and interesting features associated with those experienced moms. Different from new parents who would anxiously consult lots of books and magazines for advice and be overly concerned about what to do and what not to do with their babies, second-time moms were found to be confident (they trust their instinct and make no apologies), honest (they admit that sometimes things are not always perfect), humorous (they tend to laugh at their own mistakes rather than cry), and not judgmental (they think there is no perfect way of parenting and they believe loving their kids is what that matters). Thus, when Luvs launched its campaign to target this unique group of consumers, the theme was "By their second kid, every mom is an expert and more likely to choose Luvs. Live, Learn and Get Luvs."[20] The effects of this targeted advertising were favorable. The central piece of the advertising campaign, a 30-second commercial called "Breastfeeding," was viewed more than 2 million times on YouTube and generated thousands of comments.[21]

Message Creation

Theoretically speaking, the creation of targeted advertising messages will be based on the key consumer insights found in the research. However, there is no single universally accepted guideline with regard to how these messages should be created and delivered. As mentioned in the last chapter, the same information can be presented in very different ways and lead to significantly different effects. When creating a targeted message, you need to take all sorts of issues into consideration, such as language, celebrity, artwork, format, media channel, and so forth. In this sense, to create an ad is a work of art, not of science.

What language to use in the message may be the first thing for you to consider. If you are targeting a minority group, for example, you need to decide whether you want to use their ethnic language in the advertising. Using different languages (such as English versus Spanish) or a combination of different languages (such as English plus Spanish versus Spanish plus English) can generate very different results.[22] In a study that interviewed 648 Spanish-dominant or bilingual Hispanic consumers in Los Angeles, New York, Miami, and Houston, for instance, it was found that those consumers were more likely to be persuaded when they were exposed to commercials in Spanish, embedded in Spanish television programs, than similar commercials in English, embedded in English television programs.[23]

The reason why languages matter is because they are often associated with certain cultural meanings.[24] The dominant language (such as English) and minority language (such as Spanish) in a society may represent different levels of power or social status. However, the dominant language is not always perceived as favorable, and the minority language is not necessarily perceived as unfavorable, either.[25] It is possible that people hold favorable (or unfavorable) attitudes toward several languages, and each of them is related to a particular set of meanings. For instance, in a research study with Indian people, Hindi was found to be associated with belongingness (e.g., close, personal, friendly, and family) and English was found to be associated with sophistication (e.g., global, cosmopolitan, urban, and upper class).[26] Thus, you should be careful in selecting the language in your advertising. It needs to be consistent with the expectation of your target consumers.

In addition to language, you also need to think of other elements in the advertising message such as the model to be used, the artwork, and so forth. For example, consumers in your target group may have a similar level of reading. That will determine how many technical terms or laymen language you want to use in the ad. They may also have similar taste in color and graphics, and common preferences for a specific type of model or testimonial.[27] If you are targeting a specific ethnic group, there are a full range of communication tools that you can use, such as music, celebrities, artwork, traditional dresses, national flags and holidays, and so forth.[28] The key is to choose the right tool to establish a connection between the brand and the target consumers.

I will use two of my studies to explain how different models and artwork can produce different persuasion effects for the same brand or product. In one study, my coauthor and I tested the effects of advertising with three types of models with 155 Hispanic consumers from an online consumer panel: non-Hispanic White models only, Hispanic models only, both non-Hispanic and Hispanic models.[29] Although the product promoted in the ad was the same, people evaluated the advertising message differently when it featured different models. Those who were highly assimilated to the mainstream American culture showed the most favorable attitude toward the ad with non-Hispanic White models only, but people who were strongly connected to the ethnic Hispanic culture preferred the ad with Hispanic models only. The third type of individuals, who embraced the two cultures, liked the ad with both non-Hispanic and Hispanic models the best.

In another study, I tested the effects of product package with 251 Chinese consumers in Miami (product package is a special case of advertising).[30] Four versions of artwork were put on the package of the same product (a chocolate bar) for testing purposes: American cultural icons (Capitol Hill plus the Statue of Liberty), Chinese cultural icons (the Temple of Heaven plus Confucius), bicultural icons (the Statue of Liberty and Confucius), and non-cultural icons (rectangle and circle). An interesting finding of the study was that people were willing to pay a significantly higher price for the product when the package featured both American and Chinese cultures (the average was $5.38) than when it featured American culture only (the average was $3.48) or Chinese culture only (the average was $3.20).

Moreover, the format of presenting an advertising message also influences its effects. I will use one of my favorite advertising campaigns to illustrate this point. The campaign was implemented by Audi in 2005 when it started to launch the new A3 model, and it was named "Art of the heist." After a careful examination of consumer research data (the A3 was targeting young and affluent male individuals in the United States), Audi discovered an important commonality among their target consumers: mystery. Those consumers liked to play games and they preferred a great deal of intellectual challenge. Based on these findings, Audi presented its advertising message in a very intriguing and nontraditional way—"alternate reality branding."[31] It started with an Audi A3 theft at a New York City dealership, and followed by Audi's handbills seeking information about the theft. Later on, the whole campaign evolved into a three-month-long and 24/7 reality game. Consumers did not just watch the story unfold, but they actually played a role in it!

However, very few campaigns can be implemented in such an innovative way like "Art of the heist." In fact, Audi had to employ a full-time lawyer as part of the advertising team because the campaign involved so many risky elements.[32] Most targeted advertising campaigns today are still conducted in a traditional way and advertising messages get delivered through conventional mass media. That is to say, to select the right media channel for your targeted message is an important consideration. Consumers who prefer different media tend to differ in many other aspects as well although they may share common demographic characteristics or geographic location.[33] Here I will use MRI+ database again as an example to explain how to choose the right media for targeted messages. For instance, in the database when I search for those consumers who are more likely to consume energy drinks, it turns out that men aged between 18 and 34 may be the target group that I am looking for (they are 104 percent more likely to consume energy drinks than the general public). Now I need to find out what possible media vehicles I may use to target them. The database shows a bunch of options including cable, magazine, radio, and website. Based on the data, the magazine *4-Wheel & Off-Road* seems to be a possible choice (among several others) since people who read this magazine show a very high tendency to drink energy drinks!

Chapter Summary

The key takeaways of this chapter are summarized as follows:

- To adopt the targeted advertising strategy, your product or service should have a clear and distinctive appeal to a particular group of consumers (the target group). Essentially, you want people in the target group to associate themselves and their peers with your brand.
- There are multiple ways to select the target consumer group (it is a process of market segmentation), including demographic segmentation, geographic segmentation,

psychographic segmentation, behavioral segmentation, and so forth. It is up to you to decide what consumer group to target for your business. In some cases, this decision may be arbitrary.

- In a targeted communication process, the consumers will expect a certain level of variation of message or choice. They should easily recognize that the advertising message is not about a standardized product or service, but something particularly relevant to their group.

- To implement the targeted advertising strategy, you do not need to set up a database containing each individual consumer's features and characteristics. However, you do need to conduct research to find out the common characteristics consumers in the target group share.

- When creating a targeted advertising message, you need to take all sorts of issues into consideration such as language, celebrity, artwork, format, media channel, and so forth. You must ensure that the message you create is relevant to the target group and helps the target consumers enhance their group identity.

CHAPTER 5

How Does Individualized Advertising Strategy Work?

This chapter provides a detailed description of the individualized advertising strategy and further explains when this strategy should be adopted and how it should be implemented. Specifically, it answers the following questions:

- What core business values a company should have if the individualized advertising strategy is adopted?
- What expectation the consumers should have from the company if the individualized advertising strategy is adopted?
- What consumer insights should be generated from research to implement the individualized advertising strategy?
- How should an individualized advertising message be created?

When Is Individualized Strategy Needed?

Proposition of Your Business Value

Both the standardized and targeted strategies can be considered as traditional ways of doing advertising. Most companies today are still using either one of those two types of strategies. The third option, the individualized strategy, is a newcomer into this domain. It has attracted wide attention from both academia and practitioners during the past decade, largely due to the rapid development of Internet technologies. High-technology companies such as Amazon, Google, and Facebook have shown success in adopting such a strategy, but is it the right choice for your business?

Contrary to the standardized strategy that neglects the market heterogeneity and assumes consumers share common needs and wants, the individualized strategy considers each consumer's unique preferences to the fullest extent. The objective of an individualized communication is to treat each consumer as a special person by sending a unique message to him or her. The whole marketplace consists of millions of consumers. To implement the individualized strategy, it means that you need to create millions of different messages based on each consumer's unique preferences. As you can imagine, this is not an easy task. You should carefully evaluate your core business value before jumping on the bandwagon of individualization. Whether your company is suitable for the individualized strategy is fundamentally dependent on two conditions: whether each consumer in your industry has a unique demand, and whether your company is capable of fulfilling each person's unique demand at the same time.

First, you need to evaluate the nature of your industry and figure out whether individualization is suitable for it. In some industries, consumers' demands are highly similar and therefore, it is unnecessary to individualize the communication process between the company and each consumer. As mentioned in Chapter 3, such examples include gasoline, salt, and so forth. However, in other industries, consumers' demands may be so fragmented that each one differs from another. In this case, if a company can develop an individualized communication process to cater to these unique preferences, it is likely to be appreciated. Amazon (www.amazon.com), the largest online bookseller (it is also an online retailer of many other things), is a good example to illustrate this point because consumers' preferences of books tend to be unique and inimitable. Compared to a physical bookstore where consumers may or may not find the exact book they want, Amazon hosts a large online inventory where people can find almost any book. This online setting has certainly changed the way consumers buy and read books. It looks much more convenient for a person to buy books online and have them delivered to his or her home or directly downloaded to his or her digital device than to drive to a physical bookstore. In fact, this change of consumers' shopping habit is the primary reason why Borders, the second-largest U.S. bookstore chain, went out of business in 2011.[1] When Borders started its business over 40 years ago, it stocked rich assortments of books that competitors could not match. However, the company failed to modify its business model to adapt to the digital era and eventually lost its business.[2]

Second, whether your company should adopt the individualized strategy depends on whether you have enough technology capability to handle each consumer's unique demand at the same time. Amazon does a great job in remembering each person's purchase history and recommending something relevant when he or she logs in the second time, owing to the company's technology sophistication.[3] Can a physical bookstore do that? Well, maybe a bookstore employee can remember 20 to 50 consumers who frequently stop by. However, it will be extremely difficult for him or her to remember thousands of consumers and recommend something special for each of them accordingly. From this perspective, technology is the real driver of individualization. Without a strong information technology department, you probably won't be able to implement the individualized strategy.

As a matter of fact, high-technology companies are continuously updating their technologies to make an individualized communication more powerful. For instance, Amazon was recently granted a patent for what it called anticipatory shipping, a technology that allows the company to deliver product packages even before consumers order them.[4] Sounds like a fairy tale, doesn't it? The truth is: Amazon knows the consumers so well by tracking each of them online. The company can predict what a person is likely to buy based on his or her previous purchases, product searches, returns, and even how long the cursor hovers over an item on its website.[5] Another example is a technology called predictive search, developed by Google and other companies. This is a cell phone application (such as Google Now) that anticipates what a person needs before he or she even asks for it.[6] For instance, it will alert a person that he or she needs to leave early for the next meeting because of the traffic although the person never told his or her phone that he or she had a meeting or where the meeting was. How is this possible? Again, it is the power of technology. The cell phone application actually reads the user's e-mail, scans his or her calendar, tracks his or her location, parses the traffic patterns, and then anticipates what he or she needs before he or she himself even knows.[7]

Expectation of Your Consumers

Since differences in needs and preferences drive people to seek individualized information, product, and service, precisely understanding consumers' expectation of your company is very important for your individualized strategy to succeed.[8] Generally speaking, today's consumers are more powerful and active than before because of the Internet and social media. They are the center of business communications and their voices can sometimes change business operations. How to live up to the consumers' expectation is becoming a critical component of a company's core decisionmaking.

There are many examples to illustrate this argument. For instance, consumers nowadays can participate in the process of determining the price of a product or service. They can go to Priceline (www.priceline .com) to propose a price that they are willing to pay for a hotel, a flight, or a rental car. The website will accommodate such requests and negotiate the price for them. In another example, Bank of America decided to drop its plan of charging a five-dollar monthly fee for debit-card users due to massive customer concerns expressed online—a 22-year-old girl named Molly Katchpole initiated a petition online (www.change.org) and it was later joined by more than 300,000 people.[9] Let's face it. Ten or fifteen years ago, companies probably would not have proactively asked their consumers what price they were willing to pay. They probably would not worry much about one consumer being unsatisfied with their business plan, either. However, the Internet gives people an opportunity to connect with each other and express a collective feeling. When the feeling is negative, if the company does not react quickly, it can turn into a public relations nightmare. For example, in 2009 United Airlines refused to pay $1,200 to Dave Carroll, a Canadian musician, for the repair of his guitar which was broken by the baggage handlers.[10] After several months of unsuccessful communication with United Airlines' customer service department, the musician eventually expressed his anger in a dramatic way—he wrote a song about his bad experiences with the company (the song was named United Breaks Guitars) and put his music video on YouTube.[11] As of February 2014, the video has been viewed more than 13 million times and generated over 25,000 comments!

As reflected in the examples mentioned earlier, consumers are no longer passive message receivers in a communication process in today's digital era. Their expectation of how companies should design and manufacture a product, provide a service, and deliver a message has significantly increased, especially in some industries. A good example to demonstrate how consumers' expectation rises from a standardized communication to an individualized communication is the newspaper industry. In the past, newspapers had always been produced in a standardized way and consumers were fine reading the same new stories as others. However, the Internet has changed the game completely. Since the early 1990s, a large amount of news content has appeared online. As a result, people don't rely on traditional media for news anymore because they can easily access news stories online. In fact, more Americans are now getting their news from the Internet than from newspapers or radio.[12] There are many websites that allow them to select the news that they prefer to read, such as MyYahoo! (my.yahoo.com), Google News (news.google.com), and so forth. People seem to like these individualized news sources. In a study that tested how people responded to the news content on MyYahoo!, for example, it was shown that the website generated much more favorable attitudes from consumers when it presented individualized news related to their preferred movies, sports teams, and tourist destinations than when it presented standardized information.[13]

Facebook is another great example to show how much individualization people expect in terms of receiving news nowadays. I recently conducted a survey on campus at my university with hundreds of undergraduate students, focusing on how they used Facebook to receive information. Guess what? The average number of friends those students had on Facebook turned out to be more than 800! Given that a person may get news feeds on Facebook from over 800 unique sources every day, the communication process between users and Facebook is highly individualized indeed.

Essentially, it is the development of technology that has raised the bar and increased consumers' expectation of individualization. In the old days, when people went to a library, they would browse the index cards or ask a librarian to locate some information. In general, they wouldn't expect the librarian to immediately show them the book or magazine that they were looking for. However, when people go to Google (www.google .com) to search for something today, they normally expect the website to return the exact information that they want. This information search is so individualized that it is not only based on what the search query is about, but also based on who enters the query. For example, when a person searches for "food in Boston," Google may present a blog post about restaurants in Boston written by one of his or her acquaintances as a search result.[14] It is called personalized search.

Would consumers eventually expect all communications to be individualized? Well, that may be possible, depending whether technology will be ready. However, at least for now, consumers don't expect a high level of individualization in all industries. Using higher education (the industry that I am in) as an example, the majority of university students are still getting their education in a standardized or targeted format—that a professor lectures to a room full of students with somewhat similar backgrounds and gives everyone the same test for an evaluation purpose. Students also expect a standardized form of recognition—to receive standardized letter grades from the classes they take and to receive a standardized diploma from the university they attend. Such an expectation won't change until one day all the lectures and tests can be effectively presented online.[15] It is certainly up for debate whether a standardized or individualized education system is more beneficial to students, but at least we haven't reached that point yet.

I also want to point out that a high level of individualization may not be suitable for all consumers. Several studies in the literature have shown that a highly individualized product or message may not generate a more favorable effect than a standardized or targeted product or message for consumers with some specific personality characteristics such as those who don't want to be too unique (people who tend to score low on a psychological measurement called "need for uniqueness")[16] or those who are more collectivistic-minded (people who tend to score high on a psychological measurement called "collectivistic tendency").[17] These findings were built on two theoretical foundations: need for uniqueness and individualism or collectivism. According to need for uniqueness theory,[18] all individuals crave for a certain extent of uniqueness, but there are dispositional differences among people in regard of how different they want to be from others. At one extreme, some people desire to be just like everybody else, while at the other extreme, some people want to be as unique as possible. Possessing a scarce product, for example, provides people a vehicle to establish their uniqueness.[19] In a study that examined how consumers evaluated their self-designed cell phone cover, it was found that those with a high need for uniqueness valued this individualized product more favorably than a standardized product, while those with a low need for uniqueness did not show such a preference. Furthermore, from a cultural psychology perspective, people tend to have different cultural orientations.[20] The most discussed cultural dimension in the literature is the individualism or collectivism dimension.[21] An individualistic person tends to regard himself or herself to be independent from other people, while a collectivistic person tends to consider himself or herself to be interdependent with the social group that he or she belongs to. In a study that examined how people responded to targeted and individualized advertising messages, it was found that collectivistic individuals were likely to evaluate a targeted ad more favorably than an individualized ad because of their interdependent self-identity.[22] Such a phenomenon was especially salient when the product featured in the advertising message was something used in public (such as a cell phone) rather than in private (such as a mattress).

How to Craft an Individualized Message

Consumer Insights

To implement the individualized strategy, you must set up a database at each consumer's individual level. Among the three types of strategies (standardized, targeted, and individualized), the volume and accuracy of data required by the individualized strategy is no doubt the highest. Conducting traditional secondary research and primary research won't be enough for you to establish such a database because data from those research activities cannot show each individual consumer's characteristics or preferences (they can only suggest the preferences shared by the general public or a specific group of consumers). Thus, you need alternative methods (likely to be more sophisticated as well) to collect consumer data. You also need to update the database on a regular basis.

It is worth noting that the database you set up may be a consumer database (a database containing information of people who have or haven't done business with your company) or a customer database (a database containing information of people who have done business with your company), depending on who you intend to communicate with in the advertising. Theoretically speaking, you should set up a consumer database because a prospective consumer today may become a customer tomorrow (and vice versa). As a matter of fact, to identify and differentiate consumers is believed to be the most fundamental step for the individualized strategy.[23]

Your database should contain many details about each consumer such as his or her demographics, attitudes, preferences, past behavior, and so forth. Generally speaking, these data can be acquired either explicitly or implicitly. On the one hand, you may explicitly encourage consumers to provide their information to you via some written forms (such as asking a consumer to fill out an inquiry card). On the other hand, you can implicitly record their information on your website (such as tracking a consumer's purchase history online).

The record of a consumer's actions online is known as clickstream data.[24] These data may include a record of every website and every web page seen, the time the consumer spent on each site or page, and the order the sites and pages were visited. They may also include information regarding what virtual communities the consumers had participated in, what banner ads they had clicked on, what products they had purchased.[25] In addition to these numerical data, you may sometimes even need to record textual data on the Internet such as blogs, chat forums, and virtual communities.[26]

The development of Internet technologies allows companies to collect such big data from consumers. However, it needs to be pointed out that it is often beyond the capability of a market analyst or advertising account planner to sort and analyze these data and predict what consumers will prefer (or need) in the future. You should have some information specialists run sophisticated filter algorithms for this purpose.

Message Creation

After collecting consumer data, the next step is to incorporate each consumer's characteristics or preferences in creating a message for him or her.[27] The fundamental idea of this individualization process is to produce a message that captures some facets of the message recipient's self-identity such as his or her values, experiences, and attitudes.[28]

There are many different ways to create an individualized message. The simplest approach is to add some cues to the message such as the message receiver's name.[29] These cues don't really change the content of the message, but it gives people an impression that the message is meant for them. However, it is worth noting that adding a person's name to the message may not be strong enough to make the message persuasive. For example, in a study that compared the effects of standardized and individualized newsletters (both newsletters had the same layout and provided the same information, and the only difference was that the message recipient's first name was mentioned in the individualized version but it was not in the standardized version); there were no significant differences between the two versions regarding people's attention and attitudes toward the message.[30]

More sophisticated ways of individualization include the use of a person's habits, ideology, personality, or past behavior to create the message. I will use a few examples in the literature to show how an individualized message can be produced in these ways. For instance, in a study that examined the effects of individualized news recommender systems, research participants' political ideology was measured, and then they were presented with news stories recommended by an online system.[31] A recommendation was considered as individualized if the source of those news stories appeared to be consistent with the person's political party affiliation or political ideology (e.g., self-identified Democratic or more liberal participants were recommended stories from MSNBC, and self-identified Republican or more conservative participants were recommended stories from Fox News). In another study that tested how students reacted to different types of recruitment messages, their job expectation was measured via a questionnaire from many aspects such as expected salary, number of days of training, vacation, travel supplied by the job, and so forth.[32] An individualized job posting, in this case, would reflect a person's specific job expectation. For example, for a student who expected to receive a starting salary below $30,000, the recruitment message would be deemed as individualized if it said, "We offer our associates a salary starting at $35,000. This salary appears to be greater than your expected salary."

An individualized message may not only reflect a person's habits or preferences, but also his or her personality. According to a study that examined how different message styles could lead to different persuasion effects, the same information can be phrased as dominant (by incorporating strong language consisting of assertions and commands) or submissive (by incorporating weak language consisting of questions and suggestions).[33] It was shown that dominant messages were more persuasive to consumers with a dominant personality while submissive messages were more persuasive to people with a submissive personality.

Moreover, individualized messages can be created based on a person's past behavior. In a study that focused on the topic of how to encourage households to save energy, different types of messages were created and tested for their persuasion effects.[34] Specifically, an individualized message was based on the household's past energy-saving behavior. For example, it would suggest households who indicated setting the thermostat at 23°C (73°F) in the wintertime to lower it and show how much energy they would save by doing so, but it wouldn't make such a suggestion to households who indicated setting the thermostat at 18°C (64°F). In another study that discussed how to prevent college students from binge drinking, individualized advertising messages were created and tested.[35] Research participants filled out a survey questionnaire that assessed their typical weekly drinking behavior including number of times a week they drank and the average number of drinks per occasion. A computer software was used to calculate approximately how many calories each person consumed and how much money they spent in a year, and an individualized message would include those figures (such as "Based on the information you provided about your drinking behavior, you spend about $... and consume ... calories in a year due to alcohol. Save your looks and your wallet").

As seen in all these examples, individualization essentially is to create a match between a message and certain characteristics of the message recipient.[36] A matched message tends to be more persuasive than a mismatched message because people are likely to scrutinize the message more carefully and give it more thought. However, it needs to be noted that consumers' expectation for an individualized message is generally much higher than a standardized or targeted message because they would expect an individualized message to perfectly match his or her needs and wants.[37] If the message fails to create this perfect match, its persuasion effects will be significantly jeopardized.

Chapter Summary

The key takeaways of this chapter are summarized as follows:

- To adopt the individualized advertising strategy, two conditions need to be satisfied: each consumer in your industry has a unique demand, and your company is capable of fulfilling each consumer's unique demand at the same time.
- Today's consumers are more powerful and active than before because of the Internet and social media. In general, consumers expect a high level of individualization in some industries. When receiving an individualized message, they expect the message to perfectly match their needs and wants.
- To implement the individualized advertising strategy, you need to set up a database containing each individual consumer's features and characteristics. The database should contain many details about each consumer such as his or her demographics, attitudes, preferences, past behavior, and so forth.
- Technology is the real driver of individualization because the volume and accuracy of consumer data required by the individualized advertising strategy is extremely high. Without a strong information technology department, you probably won't be able to do individualized advertising.
- There are many different ways to create an individualized advertising message. The fundamental idea is to produce a message that captures some facets of the message recipient's self-identity such as his or her values, experiences, and attitudes.

CHAPTER 6

How to Gather Consumer Insights for Advertising

This chapter explains how to use various research methods to discover consumers' preferences. It also discusses why a company needs to know the consumers at an appropriate level. Specifically, it answers the following questions:

- What kind of research data are needed for standardized advertising and targeted advertising?
- What kind of research data are needed for individualized advertising?
- What are the two ways of incorporating consumers' preferences in individualized advertising?
- Why does a company need to know the consumers well for its advertising purpose?
- Why cannot a company know the consumers too well for its advertising purpose?

Knowing Consumers' Preferences Is Critical

Short-Term Knowledge of Your Consumers

No matter what advertising strategy you decide to implement, knowing your consumers is a must. To create effective standardized or targeted messages, you need to conduct research, either qualitative or quantitative, or both, to gain some short-term knowledge of the consumers. Qualitative research methods frequently used in advertising practices include interviews, focus groups, and ethnographic observations. These types of research are not statistics-based, and they don't require a large sample size.

In contrast, quantitative research is primarily number-driven. The two commonly used quantitative research methods by advertising professionals are surveys and experiments. The sample size required for quantitative research is generally larger, thus the research findings may be generalizable.

Specifically, interviews are often conducted in a one-on-one setting. Approximately 20 to 25 interviews are needed for you to find some key consumer insights. Theoretically speaking, the consumers being interviewed should have different backgrounds so that they can reasonably represent the general public or the target group that you are interested in. Each interview may last about 30 to 45 minutes. The interview questions should be constructed in a way that they give interviewees much free space to express their experiences, stories, attitudes, feelings, emotions, and so forth. Some projective tests may also be included in the interview questions such as sentence completion (the interviewee is asked to complete a broken sentence), photo sorting (the interviewee is asked to sort photos into various groups according to a certain criterion), and consumer drawing (the interviewee is asked to draw a picture based on a question). The objective of such tests is to delve below consumers' surface responses and obtain their deep feelings, attitudes, and motivations.

Similar to interviews, focus groups are also based on oral conversations. However, this type of research is conducted in a group context instead of a one-on-one setting. Generally speaking, a focus group consists of seven or eight consumers who sit along a roundtable and talk about their experiences and attitudes. They answer questions from a focus group moderator and also interact with each other by commenting on others' responses. Such group dynamics are the key difference between a focus group and an interview. A focus group session usually lasts about an hour or an hour and a half. In order to gain more accurate consumer insights, multiple focus group sessions are oftentimes needed.

The third option of doing qualitative research is ethnographic observation. It means that you, as the researcher, go to a field (such as a bar, an event, a person's home, his or her blog, diary, journals, social media accounts, and so forth) to observe consumer behavior. The purpose of this type of research is to discover what consumers do in a natural setting without interrupting them or asking them questions. Surely, you need to carefully select whom to observe in the field. The persons selected for observation should represent the general public or the target group.

Qualitative research can give you lots of in-depth information on how consumers feel, prefer, and act, but those research findings usually cannot be generalized because the sample size is too small. To compensate for this shortcoming, you can also conduct quantitative research such as surveys and experiments. The sample size needed for a survey is between 1,000 and 1,500, roughly speaking, if you want to keep the sampling error reasonably low (a three percent sampling error or less is generally considered ideal). The questions on your survey questionnaire should mostly be numerical measures (that means you will be able to perform statistical analyses with the data). You can implement your survey in several different ways: by mail, by telephone, face-to-face, or online. If you need to create multiple versions of the questionnaire based on different languages (English and Spanish, for instance), you should follow a process called "back translation." You can create your questionnaire in English first, and then ask a bilingual person to translate the English questionnaire into Spanish. Later, you will ask another bilingual person to translate the Spanish questionnaire back into English. When you compare the two English versions of the questionnaire, one before the translation and one after, there shouldn't be any main discrepancy (if you do see a discrepancy, you need to modify the questionnaire accordingly).

Finally, you can conduct experiments to detect consumer preferences. The idea of experimental research is to test how consumers react to different treatments. For example, if you consider hiring a celebrity to endorse your brand but you are uncertain of which one may be more appropriate (you have two choices, A and B), you can design a simple experiment to help guide your decision. Specifically, you will create two versions of an advertising message, one featuring the celebrity A and the other featuring the celebrity B. Then, you invite several target consumers to the research and randomly divide them into two groups (each group usually needs 25 to 30 people). Each group will be exposed to one version of the ad, and people in the group will evaluate the advertising message that they see on a numerical scale. Based on a statistical analysis that compares the two groups, you draw a conclusion on which celebrity is more effective in promoting your brand (whichever gets a significantly higher score on the average evaluation).

I will use a few examples from recent award-winning advertising campaigns to illustrate how consumer research is conducted in the real world. The first example is Honda's "The social activity vehicle" campaign for its CR-V.[1] In this case, the advertising professionals conducted focus groups first. Then, they selected a few focus group participants and followed them on Facebook, Twitter, and other social media platforms. Those consumers were observed in a natural environment, and their feeds and posts on social media were examined and analyzed, leading to the advertising professionals' conclusions on their preferences of lifestyles, values, attitudes, and so forth.[2]

The second example is from Nike. To help develop and promote an iPhone application for NikeiD, Nike conducted a national blog and mobile phone journal study among 25 target consumers.[3] The company asked those consumers to experience the customization feature of NikeiD, blog about their life, and answer daily questions about the customization of shoes and fashion. According to the research, the advertising team discovered two key consumer insights: people who customized shoes tended to use their custom item to socially connect with others, and their customization was fueled by inspiration.[4]

The last example is Chobani's "A love story about yogurt" campaign.[5] Chobani found that many consumers expressed their love toward the brand in a variety of passionate ways such as writing love poems to it in their news feeds, writing blog posts about leaving their spouses for it, and serenading it on YouTube. To feature the best stories among consumers, the advertising team reached out and went to meet with several of them. The campaign was then designed based on real consumer stories—one that "an accountant from Virginia who had her Chobani stolen at work went on a mission to make sure it wouldn't happen again," and another that "a pre-med student from NY who rode his bike 80 miles just to see where his favorite yogurt was made."[6]

Long-Term Knowledge of Your Consumers

Traditional qualitative and quantitative research can provide you with valuable consumer insights that help you design a standardized or targeted message. However, to create a more individualized message, you need to gain more detailed knowledge of each consumer. Such a research process tends to be long-term oriented instead of a one-time shot. In general, learning about a consumer over time and delivering individualized information to him or her based on that learning is very challenging. It requires an excellent consumer database and superb analytical skills.[7]

Basically, you need to set up a database that describes each consumer in as many details as possible. These details may include both personally identifiable information (such as name, address, phone number, e-mail, credit card number, and so forth) and unidentifiable information (such as gender, hobbies, books read, holiday destinations, marital status, educational background, occupation, and so forth).[8] Such information can be collected in two ways: either you ask the consumers to disclose it to you, or you record it from them automatically with their permission.

To ask consumer to disclose their personal information to you, in general, is not an easy task. Many people are reluctant to share information with companies because they worry that the data can be used without their permission. However, when facing a specific choice that a company asks for personal information, people tend to do a risk–benefit evaluation in their mind (mostly at an unconscious level) before they make a decision. If the immediate benefit clearly offsets the potential risk, they are more likely to accept the loss of privacy that accompanies the disclosure of information.[9] According to this rationale, you may enhance consumers' willingness to disclose personal information in two ways: (1) to offer attractive benefits to them such as discount coupons and bonus reward points and (2) to decrease the perceived risk of information disclosure such as providing them with privacy notices that explain how their data will be handled and secured.[10]

Instead of asking them, you may also record consumers' data automatically, which is often known as online tracking. Each time a person goes to a company's website to search for something, to read something, or to buy something, his or her actions may be recorded and transformed into a database. The company then uses these data to create an individualized message for him or her later. The more frequently this person logs into the company's website, the more data he or she will give to the company. For example, Pandora (www.pandora.com) collects music preferences from more than 200 million registered users because they express their likes and dislikes of particular songs by pressing the thumbs-up and thumbs-down buttons.[11] The company also tracks via what devices people tune in the songs, for example, desktops and cell phones.[12] This online tracking is a nonstop process, thus it accumulates a large amount of information for each consumer. Generally speaking, this type of data collection is more intrusive into people's privacy than asking them to disclose their information voluntarily.

Predicting Consumers' Preferences Is Hard

Let Consumers Tell You

The main purpose of setting up a consumer database is to know each consumer better so that you can predict his or her preferences more precisely. An individualized message based on a person's preferences should be more effective than a random message. Two approaches, customization and personalization, can help you achieve this individualization purpose.

The two terms, customization and personalization, are sometimes used interchangeably in academic research and industrial reports. However, there are important conceptual differences between them. Customization means that the consumer proactively specifies one or more elements of his or her marketing mix (it can refer to a product, a price, or a message), while personalization means that companies determine, based on previously collected consumer data, what marketing mix (again, it can refer to a product, a price, or a message) is the most suitable for each individual consumer.[13] In other words, in a customization process consumers play an active role in defining a product, a price, or a message, but in a personalization process they don't.

Many companies have used a customization process to design and produce their products because they want consumers to tell them exactly what they prefer. For example, Dell allows consumers to customize many features of their computer such as the operating system, screen size, processor, memory, hard drive size, and so forth, when they order online (www.dell.com). For another example, the website MixYourOwnGranola (www.mixyourowngranola.com) gives consumers a chance to mix their own granola by selecting different nuts, seeds, dried fruits, and other ingredients.

In addition to designing and producing a product for a consumer, this customization logic can also be applied to creating a message for him or her. For instance, you can ask consumers to fill out a couple of short forms online by indicating what content categories they would be mostly interested in.[14] Then, you can create e-mail newsletters based on those indicated preferences. This type of individualized e-mail message is generally more effective to catch people's attention and lead to clicks compared to standardized messages.[15]

Let You Tell Consumers

If you don't want to bother your consumers and ask them what they prefer, you can use the personalization approach to create individualized messages—using the data that you have collected to predict what consumers would prefer in the future and create messages accordingly. Generally speaking, you need to have strong capabilities in statistical modeling to analyze consumer data.[16]

A central part of personalization is to predict what people would do or what they would like without directly asking them. Such a prediction is often built on an assumption or a logical inference. For example, a common personalization practice used by companies is to greet consumers by their names when sending mails or e-mails to them. It is assumed that people would prefer to see their own names rather than a generic greeting. It sounds intuitive, but in fact there is scientific evidence to support such an assumption. In two psychological experiments conducted in the 1980s, research participants were exposed to the letters of their names as well as other random letters.[17] It was found that their attitudes toward the letters of their names were significantly more favorable than toward the random letters.

Another common practice of personalization is one where companies provide offers to consumers that are consistent with their past purchases. It is assumed that people would repeat their purchases (buy the same product or a similar product) after they develop habitual patterns.[18] Again, this assumption is supported by scientific evidence. For example, in a study that tested behavioral consistency of choosing computer terminals in a lab, it was found that people would always go to his or her favorite few terminals although all computers in the lab were essentially the same.[19]

Moreover, companies sometimes can draw conclusions on consumers' interests or preferences based on logical reasoning. For example, transaction data may be used to make inferences of price sensitivity.[20] Depending on how frequently a person responded to discount offers in the past, companies may judge how sensitive he or she is to a price change. For another example, clicking on the Help button on a website may signal a person's low expertise on a certain subject.[21]

However, I must point out that these assumptions and reasoning sometimes can go wrong. It is very difficult to anticipate consumers' preferences 100 percent accurately even if you track their behavior online all the time. For instance, a consumer is likely to buy a book for himself or herself based on his or her own interests, but he or she may also use the same website to buy a book as a gift to a friend based on the friend's interests.[22] In this case, predicting this person's preferences based on the transaction data may not lead to a sound judgment.

Dos and Don'ts

Do Know Your Consumers Well

No matter what assumption or reasoning you use to predict consumers' preferences, the data that you rely on must be accurate. That is to say, maintaining and updating your consumer database is extremely important. You need to ensure that there is no misinformation in the database and consumers' status changes (such as the change of name, address, phone number, or occupation) are appropriately reflected. A tiny error in the data can ruin your whole effort in the individualized communication process. For example, in one of my studies (the study results have not been published in a journal yet), I examined how people would respond to misinformation in an ad. I created two versions of ads for my research participants, one that greeted them by their first name in the message (such as Hi Dave...) and the other that greeted them by a wrong name (such as Hi Taylor... but the person was not named Taylor). It was found that people's attitude toward the ad with the wrong name was much more unfavorable than the one with the right name, even though the brand and product information in both versions of ads was the same.

To keep the consumer database accurate and updated requires lots of hard work—the data need to be checked and examined constantly. The collaboration between different departments in a company is also critical in this sense. For example, the marketing department of a company may be in charge of the consumer loyalty program, thus they have the data that consumers filled out on the loyalty cards. On the other hand, the finance department may manage consumers' purchase data. To make the company's marketing communication more effective, the two departments need to share data with each other.[23]

Don't Know Your Consumers Too Well

Even if you have an excellent consumer database in hand, it doesn't mean that you will always be successful in the communication process. Sometimes you may run into a trouble for knowing your consumers too well. That is to say, people may not like to see a message from a company that gets too personal, which suggests that the company is inappropriately familiar with his or her preferences and behavior. This type of highly individualized messages may be irritating because they cause consumers to experience something called "psychology reactance"—a motivational state activated when a person feels his or her freedom is threatened.[24]

Simply speaking, a highly individualized message may cause people to worry about their privacy. As described by a *Time* Magazine article, a data mining company today can easily compile a huge amount of personal data about an individual consumer, pointing at every detail of his or her life—what he or she buys, where he or she goes, and whom he or she loves.[25] These data are collected in lots of ways, such as tracking devices on websites (such as cookies) that allow a company to identify a consumer as he or she travels around the Internet and applications that he or she downloads on the cell phone that look at his or her contact list and location. These data (including misinformation) are sold and used in individualizing advertising messages that are presented to each consumer.

Consumers do worry about such practices. They are concerned about their information privacy online. The perceived risk is especially high when they feel uninformed by companies about how their information is collected and used.[26] Using a consumer's real comments covered in a *New York Times* article, "It is a pretty clever marketing tool. But it's a little creepy, especially if you don't know what's going on."[27]

The reality is: consumers are not only concerned about their personally identifiable information, but also their anonymous and personally unidentifiable information, but the degree of sensitivity is different.[28] People normally consider personal identifiers (such as name, phone number, credit card number, and so forth) to be more sensitive.[29] Demographic information and personal preferences (such as gender, educational background, hobbies, and so forth) are generally regarded as less sensitive.[30] Broadly speaking, consumers' concerns for privacy regarding companies' collection and usage of their data come from four aspects: (1) companies have collected too much personal information about their consumers; (2) the personal information that companies have collected may contain errors, but they haven't devoted enough time and effort to verifying the accuracy of the data; (3) companies may use the personal information for a purpose that is not authorized by consumers who provide that information; and (4) companies' computer databases that contain personal information are not sufficiently protected from unauthorized access.[31]

If you ask a consumer whether he or she is concerned with sharing too much information with a company and losing privacy, the chances are: he or she is very much concerned. However, there is an interesting phenomenon called "privacy paradox," which means people can express a great level of privacy concern but they behave in ways that contradict their expressions.[32] A plausible explanation for such an attitude and behavior inconsistency is that people may be willing to sacrifice a certain level of privacy for a company that they trust.

Think of the following hypothetical scenario: suppose that you are busy working on a project one day and you have no time to buy lunch. All of a sudden your best friend shows up with your favorite sandwich. He tells you that he knows you are busy working on this project and he wants to help you out. Since he knows what you prefer to eat, he buys the sandwich for you. In this case, you are very likely to appreciate your friend's help. However, if a stranger shows up with the same sandwich and offers it to you, you probably won't appreciate it. Instead, you would be confused, if not scared. The first thought likely to come to your mind would be "What is going on?" or "Who are you, and how do you know what kind of sandwich I like to eat?"

The key difference between these two cases (best friend versus stranger) is the level of trust. You trust your best friend so much that you won't worry about him knowing you too well, but you certainly would not grant the same level of trust to a stranger. In fact, you probably would feel that you have been stalked by him.

As seen in this hypothetical example, building trust between your company and the consumers is very important for the communication process to succeed. A company's reputation is an asset that takes a long time to build, and people tend to rely on it to ensure that their personal information is safe.[33] The relative reputation of companies is the main reason why consumers prefer to use individualized service from one company while ignoring another, although the services may be virtually the same.[34] Just look at the list of most admired companies across the world, Apple, Google, and Amazon are ranked the top three.[35] This probably explains why consumers keep going to those companies for products and services and not worry much about privacy, although they have shared a lot of personal information with the companies.

Chapter Summary

The key takeaways of this chapter are summarized as follows:

- To create effective standardized or targeted advertising messages, you need to gain short-term knowledge of the consumers through qualitative and quantitative research. The qualitative and quantitative research methods frequently used in advertising practices include interviews, focus groups, ethnographic observations, surveys, and experiments.
- To create effective individualized advertising messages, you need to gain long-term knowledge of each individual consumer. Such consumer information can be collected in two ways: either you ask the consumers to disclose it to you, or you record it from them automatically with their permission.

- There are two ways to achieve the individualization purpose in advertising: customization and personalization. Customization means that the consumer proactively specifies what he or she prefers to see in an advertising message, while personalization means that you predict what the consumer prefers to see in an advertising message based on an analytical procedure.
- To conduct effective advertising, you need to know the consumers' preferences reasonably well. In this sense, maintaining and updating your consumer database is extremely important. You must ensure that there is no misinformation in the database.
- Consumers may experience psychological reactance if an advertising message gets too personal. To avoid such negative responses, you need to build a trustworthy relationship with the consumers. This trust-building process tends to be long-term oriented.

CHAPTER 7

How to Incorporate Consumer Insights into Advertising

This chapter discusses a few issues in the process of incorporating consumer insights into advertising. It also explains why expert and novice consumers should be differentiated in the communication process. Specifically, it answers the following questions:

- How to match an advertising message to the consumers' preferences?
- How to frame an advertising message in a persuasive way?
- How to deliver an advertising message in the right context and at the right time?
- Why should a company ask expert consumers to offer opinions on the advertising content, framing, medium, and timing?
- Why shouldn't a company ask novice consumers to offer opinions on the advertising content, framing, medium, and timing?

Incorporating Consumer Insights into Advertising Is a Headache

Matching the Content

As discussed in the last chapter, to gain short-term and long-term knowledge of the consumers is a very necessary but quite challenging task. You need to collect a lot of consumer data via appropriate research methods and establish a database accordingly. After you complete the data collection, the next step, then, is to create advertising messages based on those consumer data. This is an even bigger headache because creating right advertising messages for the consumers is very difficult. You should take three broad issues into consideration: (1) how to match the advertising content to the message recipient's preferences; (2) how to frame the advertising information in a persuasive way; and (3) how to deliver the advertising message in the right context and at the right time.

The first thing to consider is how to incorporate the consumer data into an advertising message (or, how to match the advertising content to the message receiver's preferences). You need to be very cautious with this message creation process because the consumer data that you have collected may not be reliable. Why? Well, this argument is built on the decision-making theories in consumer behavior. According to those theories, people may not have well-defined and stable preferences that they can easily retrieve from memory.[1] Thus, they tend to construct their preferences on the fly. For example, when you ask a person what color he or she prefers, the person may give you a random choice because he or she does not really have a consistent preference for a color. In this sense, what you have measured in the data collection process may not be the consumers' true preferences (in some cases, the consumers' preferences are so unstable that they may not even have true preferences). Consequently, if you create an advertising message based on those false preferences, the message is unlikely to be persuasive. This is why there are some examples like the following in the real world: a company predicts that a consumer is extremely likely to go on a European river cruise based on a sophisticated analysis of the consumer data, but in fact the person has no intention of going in that cruise.[2]

A widely cited article in the *Journal of Consumer Research* explained this phenomenon in detail.[3] It was argued that consumers don't have a master list of preferences in their memory to refer to because they lack the cognitive resources to generate well-defined preferences toward many objects. Instead, people usually construct a preference and make a choice on the spot when they have to. The specific choice that they make among several options is largely dependent on the goals that they want to accomplish at a given time. Four of the most important goals include:

(1) maximizing the accuracy of the choice; (2) minimizing the cognitive effort required to make the choice; (3) minimizing the experience of negative emotion when making the choice; and (4) maximizing the ease of justifying the decision.[4] An individual's choice in a certain scenario will likely reflect one or more of these four goals.

Such a constructive nature of consumers' preferences is very troublesome for companies to craft effective advertising messages. There is considerable psychological evidence showing that consumers may be chameleons, and their stated preferences at the time of choice tend to differ from their likes at the time of real consumption.[5] In other words, people often forecast that they would like something but subsequently discover they do not. For example, a person may buy bright red slacks anticipating that they would look festive during the winter holidays, but when the time comes to wear them he realizes that he no longer likes such an unusual style.[6]

Another argument in the literature is that people may not have good insights into their preferences, no matter whether the preferences are stable or fuzzy.[7] That is to say, people may not be able to correctly articulate what they really prefer or why they prefer certain things. For example, in the daily lives, people answer many questions about the cognitive processes underlying their choices, evaluations, judgments, and behavior, such as "Why do you like him?" and "Why did you take that job?" Interestingly, people oftentimes end up answering, "I don't know, it just came to me." This is primarily because they do not have direct access to higher order mental processes that are related to their evaluations, judgments, problem solving, and the initiation of specific behavior.[8] In such cases, people's responses to questions tend to be biased. They are likely to use some simple heuristic cues to make judgments on the spot. In a classic article published in the 1970s, a series of studies illustrated how simple cues could lead people to incorrect judgments.[9] Using one of the experiments in the article for example, research participants were asked to listen to a prerecorded message with a list of names. Two types of name lists were used in the study, with one containing 19 famous men and 20 non-famous women, and the other containing 19 famous women and 20 non-famous men. It was found that people believed there were more men in the first list and more women in the second list, even though the opposite was true. Such overestimations and underestimations observed in the experiment were due to the fact that famous names (such as Richard Nixon and Elizabeth Taylor) were easier to be recalled than non-famous names (such as William Fulbright and Lana Turner). In other words, people used the easiness of retrieving names as a simple cue to help them make judgments.

Although people's preferences tend to be constructed in many cases, it is worth noting that prior research did not suggest that the preferences are always unstable and biased. In fact, people do have relatively stable preferences for some situations. For example, a person's liking or disliking for smoking may be stable over time.[10] A nonsmoker is likely to prefer a nonsmoking room when booking a hotel. Also, consumers tend to develop more stable preferences as they gain more experiences with specific objects.[11]

Framing the Message

Suppose that your consumers have reasonably well-defined preferences and you have measured them perfectly. Now you know what content you want to include in the advertising message, but how to frame it becomes another concern. The same information framed in different ways can lead to very different communication effects. You need to determine what the most appropriate way to frame your advertising message is.

An article published in the *Journal of Communication* defined framing in the following fashion: to frame is to "select some aspects of a perceived reality and make them more salient in a communication text, in such a way as to promote a particular problem definition, casual interpretation, moral evaluation, and treatment recommendation for the item described."[12] Simply speaking, a frame will direct people's attention to particular aspects of the reality described, and simultaneously direct their attention away from other aspects.[13] Using a classic positive and negative framing case as an example, a pack of ground beef will likely be rated as better tasting and less greasy when it is labeled in a positive light (75 percent lean) rather than a negative light (25 percent fat).[14] This is because the positive labeling can lead to an encoding of the information that evokes favorable associations in memory, whereas the negative labeling of the same attribute may trigger an encoding of the information that evokes unfavorable associations.

Depending on what is framed, what is affected, and how the effect is measured, framing can be categorized into three types: (1) risk choice framing, in which the complete set of options differing in risk level is framed either positively or negatively; (2) attribute framing, in which some characteristic of an object or event is framed either positively or negatively; and (3) goal framing, in which the goal of an action or behavior is framed.[15] The most widely discussed framing effect in the literature is based on the first type—risk choice framing. It originated from a *Science* article written by two famous psychologists, Amos Tversky and Daniel Kahneman.[16] Using one of their experiments as an example, research participants were asked to make a choice between two alternate programs, both of which were aimed to prevent the outbreak of an unusual disease that was expected to kill 600 people. If program A were adopted, 200 people would be saved. If program B were adopted, there would be one-third probability that 600 people would be saved, and two-thirds probability that no people would be saved. The experiment results showed that 72 percent of research participants were in favor of program A and 28 percent of them were in favor of program B. However, people's responses were significantly changed when the framing of these two programs was different. Specifically, people were presented with another two programs: program C and program D. If program C were adopted, 400 people would die (program C was essentially the same as program A). If program D were adopted, there would be one-third probability that nobody would die, and two-thirds probability that 600 people would die (program D was essentially the same as program B). This time, the majority of research participants were in favor of program D (78 percent) instead of program C (22 percent). Apparently, the shift of people's preferences was caused by two different ways of framing the outcome. When the outcome was framed as a gain, people attempted to avoid a risk, but when the outcome was framed as a loss, they tended to take a risk.[17]

There are many such examples discussed in prior studies, suggesting all sorts of framing effects. The general conclusions based on those studies are: (1) in risky choice framing, positive frames will enhance risk aversion relative to negative frames; (2) in attribute framing, an attribute will be judged more favorably when labeled in positive terms rather than negative terms; and (3) in goal framing, a negatively framed message emphasizing losses will have a bigger impact on a given behavior than a positively framed message emphasizing gains.[18] Based on these research conclusions, you need to frame your advertising messages in a way that is supposed to produce certain communication effects you wish to see.

Delivering the Information

The last consideration is how to deliver the advertising information, such as in what context and at what time. The effectiveness of an advertising message is not only dependent on the content of the message, but also affected by situational factors.[19] For example, media context (i.e., characteristics of the content of the medium in which an ad is placed) is an important situational factor. Some types of media context may be more appropriate for certain types of advertising than others.[20] In a study that tested the effects of media context, three types of ads were selected by a jury of academics and advertising professionals for testing: humorous, warm, and rational.[21] Those ads were placed in three types of television and print contexts and presented to 314 participants. Specifically, the three television contexts included an excerpt from *The Simpsons* (a humorous television context), a gastronomic travel program situated in Italy (a warm television context), and a documentary on Egyptian pyramids (a rational television context). The three print contexts were three magazines, including one that featured cartoons, funny texts, and jokes (a humorous print context), one that featured stories and photographs evoking a warm feeling (a warm print context), and another that was composed of informative articles (a rational print context). It was found that an advertising message placed in a congruent media context (such as a humorous ad in a humorous context) tended to be perceived as more likeable when the message receiver's involvement with the product featured in the ad was low. When the person's product involvement was high, an advertising message placed in an incongruent media context, such as a humorous ad in a rational context, was likely to generate more favorable effects.

In another similar study, research participants were asked to watch a movie segment with embedded ads, and then report all the thoughts that had occurred as they watched the materials.[22] They were randomly assigned to one of the two movie clips, one that induced a positive mood (the opening scene of *Lethal Weapon 3* where good guys captured the bad guys in an amusing scenario), and the other that induced a negative mood (the opening scene of *Cliffhanger* where the hero failed to rescue a mountain climber whose safety line broke). The study results suggested that the negative-mood-inducing context led people to more thoughts of the movie content and their attention to the ads was distracted. However, the positive-mood-inducing context did not have such an effect.

In addition to the content of the medium, the medium itself is also a situational factor that may influence advertising effectiveness. For example, in a very interesting study, people's responses to advertising messages were tested in two conditions: one that a traditional medium (it referred to a newspaper in the study) held the ad, and the other that a creative medium (it referred to an egg or an elevator in the study) held the ad.[23] Specifically, in the creative medium condition, an insurance company's ad was printed on the shell of an egg that was placed in an open egg carton, and an energy drink ad was printed on a sticker that was posted between the up and down buttons on an elevator panel. These two medium choices were considered as creative and suitable because an egg's shell is a protective layer (thus it is appropriate for the brand image of an insurance company) and an elevator moves people up quickly (thus it is appropriate for the brand image of an energy drink). The study results showed that, compared to the traditional newspaper advertising, ads placed in these creative media were perceived as more credible and more favorable.

Furthermore, the timing of advertising is also critical to advertising effectiveness. For example, the effects of an ad are likely to differ if it is viewed by a consumer before the product's consumption as opposed to if it is viewed by the person after the product's consumption. In a study that tested this proposition, research participants were invited to taste orange juice.[24] Half of them reviewed and evaluated the orange juice company's ads before they tasted the product. The other half of them tasted the juice first and then reviewed and evaluated the ads. The time interval between these two tasks was also controlled in the study. Half of the participants did the two tasks immediately one after another (it was referred to as the online condition in the study), and the other half of them received a 15-minute distraction between the two tasks (it was referred to as the memory-based condition in the study). The research findings were that people's overall evaluations of the orange juice were significantly higher when the advertising preceded the tasting experience in the online condition, and when the advertising followed the tasting experience in the memory-based condition. The reason of such findings was that people's judgments in the online condition tended to rely on what was currently in their short-term memory, whereas their judgments in the memory-based condition were likely based on retrieval of information from the long-term memory.

Another interesting phenomenon in relation to the timing of advertising is called the serial position effects (they are also termed the primacy and recency effects).[25] This phenomenon refers to the fact that when people are presented with a list of items, they tend to remember the items at the beginning or the end of the list better than the items in the middle of that list. Several studies have discussed how the serial position effects can be applied to advertising practices. Using one of my research projects as an example, I adopted the primacy and recency effects framework to test consumers' memory (both brand recall and recognition) of the 2006 Super Bowl commercials.[26] A total of 489 consumers who watched the Super Bowl broadcast that year were randomly selected and surveyed via telephone. They were asked to recall and recognize the commercials aired during the broadcast. Based on the position of each commercial in a clutter and also the position of each clutter within the whole Super Bowl broadcast, I performed the data analysis at two levels. First, at the micro-level, it was found that an earlier position for a commercial in a clutter tended to generate better brand recall. At the macro-level, it was found that the commercial clutters at earlier positions within the whole broadcast generated better brand memory. Both findings confirmed a strong primacy effect.

Dos and Don'ts

Do Ask Consumers to Help

Given the fact that you need to consider the three issues mentioned earlier, creating an effective advertising message looks like a tough job and therefore sometimes, you may need your consumers to help you in this process. Specifically, you may interact with the consumers and ask for their opinions on your advertising content, framing, medium, and timing. To get consumers involved in these decision-making processes is likely to give them a sense of empowerment, which usually leads to a positive feeling. Empowered consumers usually believe that they have a stronger impact on a company than non-empowered consumers. When they are allowed to participate in a company's decision making, they tend to assume psychological ownership of those decisions.[27]

In a study that tested the effects of consumer empowerment, research participants were introduced to a company specializing in T-shirts.[28] The uniqueness of this company was that it would promote five newly designed T-shirts per week. The participants were divided into four groups in the study. People in the first group were asked to rate 20 T-shirts on attractiveness and they were informed that the company would promote five of them next week based on their ratings. Thus, these consumers were empowered. The other three groups were non-empowered control groups, serving for different comparison purposes. Specifically, people in the second group did not see those 20 T-shirts and they were told that the company would select five T-shirts to promote based on the feedback of a user community. People in the third group got to see those 20 T-shirts but they were not given an opportunity to evaluate them. Finally, people in the last group saw the 20 T-shirts and they also rated them, but they were told that the company might not use their ratings to select the five T-shirts to promote. One week later, the five selected T-shirts were presented to all participants (people in all groups were exposed to the same five T-shirts). Their willingness to pay for those T-shirts was measured through a bidding process. It was discovered that people in the first group were willing to pay a significantly higher price for the T-shirts than people in the other three groups.

Such a consumer empowerment effect is similar to the "I design it myself" effect, which suggests that people like to assign a high subjective value to his or her own creation in a self-design activity such as pottering, cooking, and knitting.[29] To apply the same logic, companies may not only ask consumers to talk about their preferences, but also invite them to actually create advertising messages. As an example, Dove conducted an Ad Makeover campaign along this line.[30] The company created a user-friendly application via which the consumers could easily design a positive ad on Facebook (a positive ad meant an ad that would promote women's self-esteem in this case) to replace a negative ad there (a negative ad meant an ad that would lower women's self-esteem in this case). To ensure that the positive ads developed by the consumers would always take the place of negative ads, Dove used a system of double bidding (which meant Dove was willing to pay a double price for a suggested keyword). The results were that in just two weeks after the campaign was launched, ads created by the consumers displaced 171 million potentially negative ads.

Don't Ask Consumers to Help

Unfortunately, consumers cannot always help you improve the advertising effectiveness. The empowerment effect is largely dependent on whether people have enough competence to make sound choices.[31] When the consumers don't have sufficient expertise to answer your questions, it is better to leave them alone. Information overload can make people feel overwhelmed and dissatisfied and eventually lose interest in your company.[32]

Research has shown that people with more experiences (experts) are eager to participate in the information flow, but people with less experience (novices) do not have such a desire. For example, in a study that examined how users responded to the interface of Google News, it was found that people who lacked the expertise and interest in adopting new technologies (they were called non-power users in the study) preferred to see that Google automatically selected news stories for them, whereas people who liked to push a technological device to its functional limit (they were called power users in the study) preferred to select the news stories by themselves.[33]

Based on this understanding, you should differentiate experts and novices among the consumers, and not ask for too much involvement from the novices. In general, novice consumers are less likely to have stable preferences and good insights into their preferences.[34] Therefore, when a consumer has an initial contact with your company (such as talking to one of your salespersons), there should be a well-defined procedure to discern whether the person is an expert or a novice (such as that the salesperson is adept to tell whether the person has stable preferences).[35] With that knowledge in mind, the communication between your company and the consumer can to be arranged accordingly—the communication can be somewhat more complex for expert consumers but it needs to be relatively simple and less demanding for novice consumers.

Chapter Summary

The key takeaways of this chapter are summarized as follows:

- Your advertising messages should be created based on the consumers' preferences. However, you need to be cautious with this message creation process because the consumers' preferences may be unstable and fuzzy. It is possible that the consumer preference data you have collected are not reliable because people tend to construct their preferences on the fly.

- The same information framed in different ways (such as risk choice framing, attribute framing, and goal framing) can lead to very different persuasion effects. Therefore, you need to frame your advertising messages in a way that is supposed to produce certain communication effects you wish to see.

- The effectiveness of your advertising messages is not only dependent on the content of the message, but also affected by other situational factors such as the media where the messages are placed and the timing of advertising.

- For expert consumers, you may interact with them and ask for their opinions on your advertising content, framing, medium, and timing. To get them involved in these decision-making processes is likely to give them a sense of empowerment, which usually leads to a positive effect.

- For novice consumers, you need to ensure that the communication process is relatively simple because they do not have sufficient expertise to answer your questions. Information overload can make them feel overwhelmed and dissatisfied and eventually lose interest in your company.

CHAPTER 8

How to Integrate Different Advertising Strategies Together

This last chapter summarizes the main arguments presented in the earlier chapters. It also concludes on how the three types of advertising strategies can be integrated together. Specifically, it answers the following questions:

- What are the good and bad of standardized advertising?
- What are the good and bad of targeted advertising?
- What are the good and bad of individualized advertising?
- What is the key element shared by all three types of advertising strategies?
- How to integrate the three types of advertising strategies together?

Good and Bad of Different Strategies

Standardized Strategy

This last chapter is about some concluding thoughts. I have laid out conceptual differences of three different types of strategies from Chapter 2 to Chapter 5. I have also discussed how to measure consumers' preferences and incorporate those data into creating advertising messages in Chapter 6 and Chapter 7. Now it is time to summarize good and bad of each strategy and draw some meaningful conclusions.

All three types of strategies can be interpreted from a market segmentation perspective, but the size of each segment differs. The standardized strategy considers the whole marketplace to be one segment with all consumers belonging to this gigantic segment. This strategy assumes that all consumers share common needs and wants, and they will respond to a standardized message favorably if it contains an attractive universal appeal. Although standardization may be regarded as an outdated strategy, it still has lots of merits.[1] To summarize what have been discussed in the past few chapters, the major advantages of standardized advertising include the following:

- Standardized advertising can save cost. To produce a standardized advertising message is generally less expensive than to produce a targeted or individualized advertising message.
- When a company's advertising is standardized, it helps keep a consistent brand image and avoid consumer confusion.
- Standardized advertising's dependence on consumer data is low. A company does not need to measure each consumer's preferences for its standardized advertising. Thus, there is little concern of invading consumers' privacy.
- There is a high potential of using standardized advertising across different media. A Super Bowl commercial, for example, can be streamed online.

However, the standardized strategy is not without shortcomings. The major disadvantages of standardized advertising include the following:

- It is often difficult for a company to find a universal appeal to use in a standardized advertising message that will be attractive to all consumers. Such an appeal tends to be a fad, and the company needs to catch it quickly.
- Since standardization is the default format of creating an advertising message, consumers are so used to this practice that it may not be eye-catching.
- Expert consumers may find standardized advertising not engaging or involving because those people oftentimes expect to control the information flow. A standardized advertising message is unlikely to evoke a feeling of control for those consumers.

- A standardized advertising message can be interpreted as a message for everybody, but it may also be interpreted as a message for nobody. Therefore, theoretically speaking, standardized advertising may be serving a segment of none (instead of a segment of all).

Targeted Strategy

The targeted strategy can be regarded as a compromise between the standardized and individualized strategy. This strategy treats the whole marketplace as several segments and each segment includes a specific group of consumers. A targeted message is designed for a selected segment, and it is supposed to reflect some common characteristics shared by all consumers in this particular segment. In summary, the major advantages of targeted advertising include the following:

- Targeted advertising may be cost efficient. In general, to create a targeted message is not as expensive as to create an individualized message.
- Similar to the standardized strategy, targeted advertising does not require the company to measure consumers' preferences at the individual level. Thus, the concern of invading consumers' privacy is low.
- The requirement of high technologies for creating a targeted advertising message is low. No sophisticated algorithm is needed for targeted advertising.
- Targeted advertising can help establish a consumer community, and enhance its unique identity.

Meanwhile, the main disadvantages of targeted advertising are the following:

- To select a specific consumer group for targeting is sometimes an arbitrary judgment. A company that adopts the targeted strategy may end up sending targeted messages to a wrong consumer group.

- Generally speaking, the consumers in a target group may be closely or loosely bounded. When the group bind is not tight, the consumers may not realize a targeted advertising message is meant for them because they are not strongly attached to the group identity promoted in the message.
- Specific targeted media may not be readily available for a targeted advertising campaign. For example, when a company wants to target a unique ethnic consumer group in a particular area, an appropriate ethnic media vehicle may not exist.
- A targeted advertising message should be created based on key consumer insights provided by representative consumers in the target group. However, it is often challenging to find such representative individuals in the consumer research.

Individualized Strategy

The individualized strategy believes that the whole marketplace is consisted of millions of segments, with each consumer being a segment. An individualized message is expected to be a unique message created for a specific consumer that reflects his or her features. From a communication effect perspective, the individualized strategy may be a double-edged sword. It may help increase the message's persuasiveness by catering to the message recipient's unique needs. However, it may hinder the communication effects by being intrusive and offensive.[2] To sum up, the major advantages of individualized advertising are as follows:

- An individualized advertising message is likely to attract people's attention because it looks more personal than a standardized or targeted advertising message.
- Individualized advertising may help a company retain its consumers because people with more experiences tend to appreciate individualized services.[3]
- Individualized advertising may also help a company build a long-term relationship with its consumers because the

company shows respect to each consumer by treating him or her in a unique way.

- If an individualized advertising message is built on a strong analytical system that can accurately predict a consumer's future preferences, it may generate an immediate consumer purchase action.

Nevertheless, individualized advertising bears its own drawbacks:

- Generally speaking, to implement the individualized advertising strategy needs a large capital investment. A company needs to have a strong information technology department to maintain a large consumer database and track each consumer's contacts with the company.[4]
- A key premise of individualized advertising is that consumers have stable preferences. They will see the value of an individualized message because the message is based on those preferences. However, in reality this may not be true in many situations. For example, a person can be a big fan of chocolate and his or her preference for a chocolate cake over other sweets may be consistent. However, he or she may still sometimes order another desert in a restaurant depending on the specific occasion.[5]
- A company needs to measure each consumer's preference for creating individualized advertising messages. Consumers' concerns for privacy can be a huge hurdle in this process. Thus, the company should be very familiar with the legislation regarding how consumer privacy ought to be protected.[6] In general, consumers are willing to share personal information with those companies that follow the right procedure and hold a good reputation.
- Novice consumers may not be able to see the true difference between an individualized message and a standardized or targeted message due to lack of experience. Individualization may not be necessary for those consumers.

Which Strategy Is Good for Your Business?

All Three Strategies Point to One Thing

The rise of the Internet in the past two decades has fundamentally changed the advertising philosophy and practices. A noticeable phenomenon is that some companies have started to create individualized advertising instead of the traditional standardized or targeted advertising, with the help of Internet technologies. Although a few of those companies such as Google, Facebook, and Amazon have been quite successful in adopting this strategy, the intuitive belief that individualized messages are always more effective than standardized or targeted messages is probably misleading.[7] Going back to the basic definition of advertising discussed in Chapter 1, advertising essentially is communication. A communication process is consisted of a message sender, a message, a medium, and a message receiver. At the end of the day, the communication effects of a message are dependent on the message receiver's subjective discretion, rather than the message sender's objective attempt. That is to say, a message sender's intention in creating a message may not be correctly translated into a message receiver's perception. For example, a company may create a funny ad and send it to many consumers. However, consumers may not necessarily perceive the message to be humorous, potentially because they don't get the joke or because they consider the joke to be offensive instead of entertaining.

Following this logic, when a company creates a standardized advertising message, consumers may not necessarily perceive the message to be standardized. Also, when a company creates an individualized advertising message, it may be misinterpreted as standardized or targeted by consumers as well. I recently completed two studies (the study results have not been published in a journal yet), and the study findings indeed supported this notion. In the first study, I compared the effects of individualized messages to targeted messages. Specifically, I measured the research participants' travel interests at the individual level (the most favorable travel destinations that they wished to go to) and the group level (the most favorable travel destinations that their peers wished to go to). Then, half of them were exposed to a promotional message that was created based on their individual travel interests (this message was meant to be an individualized message), while the other half were exposed to a similar message that was created based on their peers' travel interests (this message was meant to be a targeted message). It was found that people's attitudes toward the two versions of messages were indifferent because many of them did not perceive the first type of message to be more individualized than the second one.

In my second study, I tested the effects of individualized messages and standardized messages. Half of the research participants were exposed to two individualized ads (the two ads greeted the participants by their first names), and the rest of the participants were exposed to two standardized ads (the two ads were the same to the individualized ads except for not including the participants' names). Again, no significant difference was discovered in regard to people's attitudes toward the two versions of ads, because many of them did not regard the ads that greeted them by their names to be more individualized than those without the names.

The findings in my two studies are actually consistent with what was suggested in a recent meta-analysis. According to that meta-analysis of 57 studies on the effects of individualized messages, the overall effect size of individualization was found to be .074.[8] The term effect size contains statistical meanings. In layman's language, it refers to the strength of a phenomenon. A size of .074 implies a small effect (an effect size smaller than .1 will generally be considered as small), which means individualized messages may not outperform non-individualized messages in regard to the persuasion effects in many cases.

If the message strategy per se does not matter (such as that individualization is not always superior to standardization or targeting), what, then, really matters? The answer is personal relevance.[9] Consumers do not care what process a company uses to create advertising messages. What they do care about is whether the message is relevant to them or not. A company's advertising will likely generate favorable outcomes if it is perceived as highly relevant by the consumers, no matter whether it is based on the standardized, targeted, or individualized approach. In other words, if the message appears to be irrelevant to the message recipient, it will unlikely be persuasive. Therefore, all three types of strategies actually point to one thing, as summarized in the following:

- When a company uses standardized advertising, the key is to find a universal appeal that is highly relevant to all consumers.
- When a company uses targeted advertising, the key is to find a common characteristic that is highly relevant to all consumers in the target group.
- When a company uses individualized advertising, the key is to find a unique feature that is highly relevant to each specific consumer.

How to Integrate Three Strategies

Although the three types of strategies contain different conceptual meanings, they are not necessarily contradictory to each other. We can consider standardization and individualization to be the two poles of a continuum of strategic actions, and targeting as the mid-point.[10] The three strategies can in fact be integrated together. A company may use one strategy in a certain scenario and switch to another in a different context. For example, a pharmaceutical company may use traditional print or broadcast advertising to reach consumers and encourage them to visit the company's website where they can fill out a questionnaire about their specific concerns such as quitting smoking or increasing exercise.[11] Later on, the company can send a personalized newsletter, either printed or electronic, to each consumer by responding to his or her specific concerns. This communication process thus is a combination of the standardized strategy and the individualized strategy.

Even with the same media platform, the three types of strategies can sometimes be integrated seamlessly. Taking Twitter for example, a company can do all sorts of communication on this social media platform. When consumers go to a company's Twitter account, they get to see the same information (the company's tweets). Thus, this is a case of standardized advertising. When some consumers decide to follow this company on Twitter, they become a member of this virtual consumer community that the company sets up. From this perspective, it is a case of targeted advertising. When a consumer is involved in a direct conversation with the company on Twitter such as that the company retweets his or her message or the company replies to his or her comment, this becomes a case of individualized advertising.

No matter which media platform a company uses, the ultimate goal of its advertising is to influence people. This should be a continuous process instead of a one-time shot.[12] The company needs to understand the consumers' needs and wants, and accommodate them accordingly. In this sense, communication is a learning process, an interaction process, and also a relationship-building process. It is always beneficial for a company to listen to the consumers' voices as long as they are willing to tell. Consumers' feedback to the company's last communication effort, for example, needs to be evaluated and recorded, thus the next communication can be more effective.[13] Remember, in today's digital era, the consumers are the center of communication. No matter whether an advertising message is standardized, targeted, or individualized, it should always be centered around the consumers!

Chapter Summary

The key takeaways of this chapter are summarized as follows:

- Each advertising strategy has its own advantages and disadvantages. No single strategy is absolutely more effective than the others.
- Generally speaking, to produce a standardized or targeted advertising message is less expensive than to produce an individualized advertising message.
- Standardized advertising and targeted advertising do not depend on consumer data at the individual level, thus there is little concern of invading consumers' privacy. However, the privacy concern can be a huge hurdle for individualized advertising.
- An individualized advertising message is more likely to attract people's attention than a standardized or targeted advertising

message. It is also more likely to generate an immediate consumer purchase action.

- Consumers do not care what strategy a company uses to
  create advertising messages. What they care is whether the
  message is relevant to them. A company's advertising will
  likely generate favorable outcomes if it is perceived as highly
  relevant by the consumers, no matter whether it is based on
  the standardized, targeted, or individualized strategy.

- Although the three types of advertising strategies contain different conceptual meanings, they are not necessarily contradictory to each other. In fact, they can be integrated together
  such as that company may use one strategy in a certain
  scenario and switch to another in a different context.

Notes

Chapter 1

1. Richards and Curran (2002).
2. Lasswell (1948).
3. Richards and Curran (2002).
4. Hoffman and Novak (1996).
5. Horovitz (2013b).
6. Nielson (2013).
7. Dahlén, Rosengren, and Törn (2008).
8. Arora et al. (2008).
9. Barry, Peterson, and Todd (1987).
10. Barry, Peterson, and Todd (1987).
11. Baskin and Pickton (2003).
12. Patwardhan, Patwardhan, and Vasavada-Oza (2011).
13. Baskin and Pickton (2003).
14. Barry, Peterson, and Todd (1987).
15. Hackley (2003).
16. Baskin and Pickton (2003).
17. Crosier, Grant, and Gilmore (2003).
18. Baskin and Pickton (2003).
19. Baskin and Pickton (2003).
20. Barry, Peterson, and Todd (1987).
21. Hackely (2003).
22. Morrison and Haley (2003).
23. El-Murad and West (2004).
24. El-Murad and West (2003).
25. El-Murad and West (2004).
26. Smith and Yang (2004).
27. Smith and Yang (2004).
28. Sasser and Koslow (2008).
29. El-Murad and West (2003).
30. Smith, Chen, and Yang (2008).
31. Stone, Besser, and Lewis (2000).

32. Sasser and Koslow (2008).
33. Smith and Yang (2004).
34. West, Kover, and Caruana (2008).
35. Dahlén, Rosengren, and Törn (2008).
36. Yoo and MacInnis (2005).
37. Holbrook and O'Shaughnessy (1984).
38. Holbrook and O'Shaughnessy (1984).
39. Holbrook and O'Shaughnessy (1984).
40. Albers-Miller and Stafford (1999).
41. Petty and Cacioppo (1986).
42. Holbrook and O'Shaughnessy (1984).
43. Weinberger, Spotts, Campbell, and Parsons (1995).
44. Albers-Miller and Stafford (1999).
45. Weinberger, Spotts, Campbell, and Parsons (1995).
46. Albers-Miller and Stafford (1999).
47. Moore, Harris, and Chen (1995).
48. Holbrook and O'Shaughnessy (1984).
49. Weinberger and Gulas (1992).
50. Weinberger and Gulas (1992).
51. Weinberger, Spotts, Campbell, and Parsons (1995).
52. Spotts, Weinberger, and Parsons (1997).
53. Weinberger, Spotts, Campbell, and Parsons (1995).
54. Ruiz and Sicilia (2004).
55. Cacioppo and Petty (1982).
56. Ruiz and Sicilia (2004).
57. Raman, Chattopadhyay, and Hoyer (1995).
58. Moore, Harris, and Chen (1995).
59. Moore, Harris, and Chen (1995).
60. Ruiz and Sicilia (2004).
61. Barry (1987).
62. Weilbacher (2001).
63. Weilbacher (2001).
64. Lavidge and Steiner (1961).
65. Barry (1987).
66. Vakratsas and Ambler (1999).
67. Vakratsas and Ambler (1999).
68. Li (2010).
69. Vakratsas and Ambler (1999).
70. Vakratsas and Ambler (1999).
71. Banjo, Germano, and Johnson (2013).
72. "Effie awards judging" (n.d.).

Chapter 2

1. Wind and Rangaswamy (2001).
2. Arora et al. (2008).
3. Mattioli (2012).
4. Schmid and Kotulla (2011).
5. Okazaki, Taylor, and Zou (2006).
6. Levitt (1983).
7. Alba et al. (1997).
8. Alba et al. (1997).
9. Li and Wang (2013).
10. Smith (1956).
11. Arora et al. (2008).
12. Lampel and Mintzberg (1996).
13. Smith (1956).
14. Grier and Brumbaugh (1999).
15. "Audi: The art of the heist" (2006).
16. Grier and Brumbaugh (1999).
17. Grier and Brumbaugh (1999).
18. Holland and Gentry (1999).
19. Green (1999).
20. Holland and Gentry (1999).
21. Muniz and O'Guinn (2001).
22. Vesanen and Raulas (2006).
23. Tam and Ho (2006).
24. Arora et al. (2008).
25. Wind and Rangaswamy (2001).
26. Pandora (2014).
27. Sharma (2014).
28. Montgomery and Smith (2009).
29. Wind and Rangaswamy (2001).
30. Moon (2002).
31. De Pechpeyrou (2009).
32. Shen and Ball (2009).
33. Wogalter, Racicot, Kalsher, and Simpson (1994).
34. Heerwegh, Vanhove, Matthijs, and Loosveldt (2005).
35. Porter and Whitcomb (2003).
36. Bargh and Chartrand (1999).
37. Petty and Cacioppo (1986).

Chapter 3

1. Barbaro (2007).
2. Agrawal (1995).
3. Peppers, Rogers, and Dorf (1999).
4. Anderson (2004).
5. Anderson (2004).
6. Taylor (2009).
7. Taylor (2009).
8. Newman (2010).
9. "Bing/Decode Jay-Z case study" (2011).
10. Brown (2014).
11. Brown (2014).
12. Edwards (2012).
13. Edwards (2012).
14. Li, Sun, and Wang (2007).
15. Nudd (2013).
16. Lee (2013).
17. Reichert (2002).
18. Putrevu (2008).
19. Reichert (2002).
20. Reichert et al. (1999).
21. Reichert and Carpenter (2004).
22. Putrevu (2008).
23. Horovitz (2013a).
24. Reichert (2002).
25. Belch, Holgerson, Belch, and Koppman (1982).
26. Reichert (2002).
27. Reichert (2002).
28. Schumann, Hathcote, and West (1991).
29. Brønn and Vrioni (2001).
30. Schumann, Hathcote, and West (1991).
31. "LG: Before you text, give it a ponder" (2010).
32. "Chipotle: Cultivate a better world" (2012).

Chapter 4

1. Kreuter and Skinner (2000).
2. Moriarty, Mitchell, and Wells (2012).
3. Moriarty, Mitchell, and Wells (2012).
4. Lin (2002).

5. Boote (1984).
6. "Strategic Business Insights: US VALS™" (n.d.).
7. "Strategic Business Insights: US framework" (n.d.).
8. Potter, Forrest, Sapolsky, and Ware (1988).
9. Assael (2005).
10. Rogers (1962).
11. Li, Tsai, and Soruco (2013).
12. Wind and Rangaswamy (2001).
13. Wind and Rangaswamy (2001).
14. Goodson and Shaver (1994).
15. Holland and Gentry (1999).
16. "MRI+ Database" (n.d.).
17. "Pampers: Pancitas in concert" (2013).
18. "Pampers: Pancitas in concert" (2013).
19. "Luvs: Second time moms & the truth about parenting" (2013).
20. "Luvs: Second time moms & the truth about parenting" (2013).
21. "Luvs commercial: Breastfeeding" (2012).
22. Luna and Peracchio (2005).
23. Roslow and Nicholls (1996).
24. Hofstede (2001).
25. Li and Kalyanaraman (2012).
26. Krishna and Ahluwalia (2008).
27. Kreuter and Skinner (2000).
28. Holland and Gentry (1999).
29. Tsai and Li (2012).
30. Li (2014).
31. Kiley (2005).
32. Kiley (2005).
33. O'Guinn, Faber, and Meyer (1985).

Chapter 5

1. Spector and Trachtenberg (2011).
2. Spector and Trachtenberg (2011).
3. Tam and Ho (2006).
4. Bensinger (2014).
5. Bensinger (2014).
6. Miller (2013).
7. Miller (2013).
8. Vesanen and Raulas (2006).
9. Rattray (2011).

10. Clark (2009).
11. "United breaks guitars" (2009).
12. Gross (2010).
13. Kalyanaraman and Sundar (2006).
14. Miller (2011).
15. Koller (2011).
16. Tian, Bearden, and Hunter (2001).
17. Singelis (1994).
18. Snyder and Fromkin (1977).
19. Snyder (1992).
20. Franke and Schreier (2008).
21. Triandis (1995).
22. Kramer, Spolter-Weisfeld, and Thakkar (2007).
23. Peppers, Rogers, and Dorf (1999).
24. Bucklin and Sismeiro (2009).
25. Bucklin and Sismeiro (2009).
26. Arora et al. (2008).
27. Kramer, Spolter-Weisfeld, and Thakkar (2007).
28. Tam and Ho (2006).
29. Howard and Kerin (2004).
30. Maslowska, van den Putte, and Smit (2011).
31. Beam (2013).
32. Dineen, Ling, Ash, and DelVecchio (2007).
33. Moon (2002).
34. Abrahamse, Steg, Vlek, and Rothengatter (2007).
35. Pilling and Brannon (2007).
36. Petty, Wheeler, and Bizer (2000).
37. Wind and Rangaswamy (2001).

Chapter 6

1. "Honda: The social activity vehicle" (2012).
2. "Honda: The social activity vehicle" (2012).
3. "Nike: NikeiD iPhone app" (2010).
4. "Nike: NikeiD iPhone app" (2010).
5. "Chobani: A love story about yogurt" (2011).
6. "Chobani: A love story about yogurt" (2011).
7. Shen and Ball (2009).
8. Xie, Teo, and Wan (2006).
9. Xie, Teo, and Wan (2006).
10. Xie, Teo, and Wan (2006).

11. Singer (2014).
12. Singer (2014).
13. Arora et al. (2008).
14. Postma and Brokke (2002).
15. Postma and Brokke (2002).
16. Arora et al. (2008).
17. Nuttin (1985).
18. Murray and Häubl (2009).
19. Sundar (2004).
20. Montgomery and Smith (2009).
21. Miceli, Ricotta, and Costabile (2007).
22. Peppers, Rogers, and Dorf (1999).
23. Vesanen and Raulas (2006).
24. White, Zahay, Thorbjørnsen, and Shavitt (2008).
25. Stein (2011).
26. Jai, Burns, and King (2013).
27. Helft and Vega (2010).
28. Chellappa and Sin (2005).
29. Xie, Teo, and Wan (2006).
30. Xie, Teo, and Wan (2006)
31. Smith, Milberg, and Burke (1996).
32. Smith, Dinev, and Xu (2011).
33. Xie, Teo, and Wan (2006).
34. Chellappa and Sin (2005).
35. "World's most admired companies" (n.d.).

Chapter 7

1. Bettman, Luce, and Payne (1998).
2. Stein (2011).
3. Bettman, Luce, and Payne (1998).
4. Bettman, Luce, and Payne (1998).
5. Syam, Krishnamurthy, and Hess (2008).
6. Syam, Krishnamurthy, and Hess (2008).
7. Nisbett and Wilson (1977).
8. Nisbett and Wilson (1977).
9. Tversky and Kahneman (1973).
10. Simonson (2005).
11. Simonson (2005).
12. Entman (1993).
13. Entman (1993).

14. Levin and Gaeth (1988).
15. Levin, Schneider, and Gaeth (1998).
16. Tversky and Kahneman (1981).
17. Tversky and Kahneman (1981).
18. Levin, Schneider, and Gaeth (1998).
19. De Pelsmacker, Geuens, and Anckaert (2002).
20. De Pelsmacker, Geuens, and Anckaert (2002).
21. De Pelsmacker, Geuens, and Anckaert (2002).
22. Aylesworth and MacKenzie (1998).
23. Dahlén (2005).
24. Braun-LaTour and LaTour (2005).
25. Stewart, Stewart, Tyson, Vinci, and Fioti (2004).
26. Li (2010).
27. Fuchs, Prandelli, and Schreier (2010).
28. Fuchs, Prandelli, and Schreier (2010).
29. Franke, Schreier, and Kaiser (2010).
30. "Dove: The Dove ad makeover" (2012).
31. Fuchs, Prandelli, and Schreier (2010).
32. Huffman and Kahn (1998).
33. Sundar and Marathe (2010).
34. Simonson (2005).
35. Bharadwaj, Naylor, and Hofstede (2009).

Chapter 8

1. Syam, Krishnamurthy, and Hess (2008).
2. Van Doorn and Hoekstra (2013).
3. Bharadwaj, Naylor, and Hofstede (2009).
4. Peppers, Rogers, and Dorf (1999).
5. Bettman, Luce, and Payne (1998).
6. FTC (2012).
7. Shen and Ball (2009).
8. Noar, Benac, and Harris (2007).
9. Noar, Harrington, and Aldrich (2009).
10. Lampel and Mintzberg (1996).
11. Wind and Rangaswamy (2001).
12. Vesanen and Raulas (2006).
13. Vesanen and Raulas (2006).

References

Abrahamse, W.; L. Steg; C. Vlek; and T. Rothengatter. December 2007. "The Effect of Tailored Information, Goal Setting, and Tailored Feedback on Household Energy Use, Energy-Related Behaviors, and Behavioral Antecedents." *Journal of Environmental Psychology* 27, no. 4, pp. 265–76.

Agrawal, M. February 1995. "Review of a 40-Year Debate in International Advertising: Practitioner and Academician Perspectives to the Standardization/Adaptation Issue." *International Marketing Review* 12, no.1, pp. 26–48.

Alba, J.; J. Lynch; B. Weitz; C. Janiszewski; R. Lutz; A. Sawyer; and S. Wood. July 1997. "Interactive Home Shopping: Consumer, Retailer, and Manufacturer Incentives to Participate in Electronic Marketplaces." *Journal of Marketing* 61, no. 3, pp. 38–53.

Albers-Miller, N.D.; and M.R. Stafford. February 1999. "An International Analysis of Emotional and Rational Appeals in Services vs. Goods Advertising." *Journal of Consumer Marketing* 16, no. 1, pp. 42–57.

Anderson, M. September 13, 2004. "On the Crest of the Wave." *Adweek*.

Arora, N.; X. Dreze; A. Ghose; J.D. Hess; R. Iyengar; B. Jing; … Z.J. Zhang. December 2008. "Putting One-to-One Marketing to Work: Personalization, Customization, and Choice." *Marketing Letters* 19, no. 3–4, pp. 305–21.

Assael, H. March 2005. "A Demographic and Psychographic Profile of Heavy Internet Users and Users by Type of Internet Usage." *Journal of Advertising Research* 45, no. 1, pp. 93–123.

Audi: The Art of the Heist. 2006. http://edwardboches.com/wp-content/uploads/2012/01/art-of-heist.pdf

Aylesworth, A.B.; and S.B. MacKenzie. Summer 1998. "Context is Key: The Effect of Program-Induced Mood on Thoughts About the Ad." *Journal of Advertising* 27, no. 2, pp. 17–31.

Banjo, S.; S. Germano; and A.R. Johnson. December 22, 2013. "Traffic at Target Stores Down After Data Breach." *Wall Street Journal*, http://online.wsj.com/news/articles/SB10001424052702303290904579274382225480644

Barbaro, M. March 2, 2007. "It's Not Only About Price at Wal-Mart." *New York Times*, http://www.nytimes.com/2007/03/02/business/02walmart.html?_r=0

Bargh, J.A.; and T.L. Chartrand. July 1999. "The Unbearable Automaticity of Being." *American Psychologist* 54, no. 7, pp. 462–79.

Barry, T.E. June 1987. "The Development of the Hierarchy of Effects: An Historical Perspective." *Current Issues and Research in Advertising* 10, no. 1–2, pp. 251–95.

Baskin, M.; and D. Pickton. November 2003. "Account Planning—From Genesis to Revelation." *Marketing Intelligence & Planning* 21, no. 7, pp. 416–24.

Barry, T.E.; R.L. Peterson; and W.B. Todd. February/March 1987. "The Role of Account Planning in the Future of Advertising Agency Research." *Journal of Advertising Research* 27, no. 1, pp. 15–21.

Beam, M.A. July 2013. "Automating the News: How Personalized News Recommender System Design Choices Impact News Reception." *Communication Research,* http://crx.sagepub.com/content/early/2013/07/31/0093650213497979.full.pdf

Belch, M.A.; B.E. Holgerson; G.E. Belch; and J. Koppman. January 1982. "Psychophysiological and Cognitive Responses to Sex in Advertising." *Advances in Consumer Research* 9, no. 1, pp. 424–27.

Bensinger, G. January 17, 2014. "Amazon Wants to Ship Your Package Before You Buy it." *Wall Street Journal,* http://blogs.wsj.com/digits/2014/01/17/amazon-wants-to-ship-your-package-before-you-buy-it/

Bettman, J.R.; M.F. Luce; and J.W. Payne. December 1998. "Constructive Consumer Choice Processes." *Journal of Consumer Research* 25, no. 3, pp. 187–217.

Bharadwaj, N.; R.W. Naylor; and F.T. Hofstede. September 2009. "Consumer Response to and Choice of Customized Versus Standardized Systems." *International Journal of Research in Marketing* 26, no. 3, pp. 216–27.

Bing/Decode Jay-Z Case Study. 2011. http://www.youtube.com/watch?v=XNic-4wf8AYg

Boote, A.S. 1984. "Interactions in Psychographics Segmentation: Implications For Advertising." *Journal of Advertising* 13, no. 2, pp. 43–48.

Braun-LaTour, K.A.; and M.S. LaTour. Autumn 2005. "Transforming Consumer Experience: When Timing Matters." *Journal of Advertising* 34, no. 3, pp. 19–30.

Brønn, P.S.; and A.B. Vrioni. 2001. "Corporate Social Responsibility and Cause-Related Marketing: An Overview." *International Journal of Advertising* 20, no. 2, pp. 207–22.

Brown, M. February 3, 2014. "Super Bowl Most-Watched U.S. TV Event of All-Time With 111.5 Million Viewers." *Forbes,* http://www.forbes.com/sites/maurybrown/2014/02/03/super-bowl-most-watched-tv-event-of-all-time-with-111-5-million-viewers/

Bucklin, R.E.; and C. Sismeiro. February 2009. "Click Here For Internet Insight: Advances in Clickstream Data Analysis in Marketing." *Journal of Interactive Marketing* 23, no. 1, pp. 35–48.

Cacioppo, J.T.; and R.E. Petty. January 1982. "The Need For Cognition." *Journal of Personality and Social Psychology* 42, no. 1, pp. 116–31.

Chellappa, R.K.; and R.G. Sin. April 2005. "Personalization Versus Privacy: An Empirical Examination of the Online Consumer's Dilemma." *Information Technology and Management* 6, no. 2–3, pp. 181–202.

Chipotle: Cultivate a Better World. 2012. http://4asstrategyfestival.com/storage/ silver_Creative%20Artists%20Agency_Chipotle.pdf

Chobani: A Love Story About Yogurt. 2011. http://www.jaychiatawards.com/ documents/winners2011/bronze_gotham_chobani.pdf

Clark, N. July 29, 2009. *Airlines Follow Passengers Onto Social Media Sites*, http://www .nytimes.com/2009/07/30/business/global/30tweetair.html?pagewanted=all

Crosier, K.; I. Grant; and C. Gilmore. March 2003. "Account Planning in Scottish Advertising Agencies: A Discipline in Transition." *Journal of Marketing Communications* 9, no 1, pp. 1–15.

Dahlén, M. September 2005. "The Medium as a Contextual Cue: Effects of Creative Media Choice." *Journal of Advertising* 34, no. 3, pp. 89–98.

Dahlén, M.; S. Rosengren; and F. Törn. September 2008. "Advertising Creativity Matters." *Journal of Advertising Research* 48, no. 3, pp. 392–403.

De Pechpeyrou, P. March 2009. "How Consumers Value Online Personalization: A Longitudinal Experiment." *Direct Marketing: An International Journal* 3, no. 1, pp. 35–51.

De Pelsmacker, P.; M. Geuens; and P. Anckaert. Summer 2002. "Media Context and Advertising Effectiveness: The Role of Context Appreciation and Context/Ad Similarity." *Journal of Advertising* 31, no. 2, pp. 49–61.

Dineen, B.R.; J. Ling; S.R. Ash; and D. DelVecchio. March 2007. "Aesthetic Properties and Message Customization: Navigating the Dark Side of Web Recruitment." *Journal of Applied Psychology* 92, no. 2, pp. 356–72.

Dove: The Dove Ad Makeover. 2012. http://4asstrategyfestival.com/ storage/Gold_%20Ogilvy%20Mather%20Advertising%20London_ DoveAdMakeover_UnlockingSocialDove%201.pdf

Edwards, J. December 31, 2012. "Here's How Much it Actually Costs to Buy One of Those Times Square Billboards." *Business Insider*, http://www .businessinsider.com/what-it-costs-to-advertise-in-times-square-2012-12

Effie Awards Judging. n.d. http://effie.org/judging/overview

El-Murad, J.; and D.C. West. July 2003. "Risk and Creativity in Advertising." *Journal of Marketing Management* 19, no. 5–6, pp. 657–73.

El-Murad, J.; and D.C. West. June 2004. "The Definition and Measurement of Creativity: What Do We Know?" *Journal of Advertising Research*, 44, no. 2, pp. 188–201.

Entman, R.M. December 1993. "Framing: Toward Clarification of a Fractured Paradigm." *Journal of Communication* 43, no. 4, pp. 51–58.

Franke, N.; and M. Schreier. June 2008. "Product Uniqueness as a Driver of Customer Utility in Mass Customization." *Marketing Letters* 19, no. 2, pp. 93–107.

Franke, N.; M. Schreier; and U. Kaiser. January 2010. "The 'I Designed it Myself' Effect in Mass Customization." *Management Science* 56, no. 1, pp. 125–40.

FTC. March 26, 2012. *FTC Issues Final Commission Report on Protecting Consumer Privacy,* http://www.ftc.gov/news-events/press-releases/2012/03/ftc-issues-final-commission-report-protecting-consumer-privacy

Fuchs, C.; E. Prandelli; and M. Schreier. January 2010. "The Psychological Effects of Empowerment Strategies on Consumers' Product Demand." *Journal of Marketing* 74, no. 1, pp. 65–79.

Goodson, S.R.; and M.A. Shaver. March 1994. "Hispanic Marketing: National Advertiser Spending Patterns and Media Choices." *Journalism Quarterly* 71, no. 1, pp. 191–98.

Green, C.L. March 1999. "Ethnic Evaluations of Advertising: Interaction Effects of Strength of Ethnic Identification, Media Placement, and Degree of Racial Composition." *Journal of Advertising* 28, no. 1, pp. 49–64.

Grier, S.A.; and A.M. Brumbaugh. Spring 1999. "Noticing Cultural Differences: Ad Meanings Created by Target and Non-Target Markets." *Journal of Advertising* 28, no. 1, pp. 79–93.

Gross, D. March 1, 2010. "Survey: More Americans Get News From Internet Than Newspapers or Radio." *CNN,* http://www.cnn.com/2010/TECH/03/01/social.network.news/

Hackley, C.E. June 2003. "Account Planning: Current Agency Perspectives on an Advertising Enigma." *Journal of Advertising Research* 43, no. 2, pp. 235–45.

Heerwegh, D.; T. Vanhove; K. Matthijs; and G. Loosveldt. April 2005. "The Effect of Personalization on Response Rates and Data Quality in Web Surveys." *International Journal of Social Research Methodology* 8, no. 2, pp. 85–99.

Helft, M.; and T. Vega. August 29, 2010. "Retargeting Ads Follow Surfers to Other Sites." *New York Times,* http://www.nytimes.com/2010/08/30/technology/30adstalk.html

Hoffman, D.; and T.P. Novak. July 1996. "Marketing in Hypermedia Computer-Mediated Environments: Conceptual Foundations." *Journal of Marketing* 60, no. 3, pp. 50–68.

Hofstede, G. 2001. *Culture's Consequences: Comparing Values, Behaviors, Institutions, and Organizations Across Nations.* Thousand Oaks, CA: Sage Publications.

Holbrook, M.B.; and J. O'Shaughnessy. Summer 1984. "The Role of Emotion in Advertising." *Psychology & Marketing* 1, no. 2, pp. 45–64.

Holland, J.; and J.W. Gentry. Spring 1999. "Ethnic Consumer Reaction to Targeted Marketing: A Theory of Intercultural Accommodation." *Journal of Advertising,* 28, no. 1, pp. 65–77.

Honda: The Social Activity Vehicle. 2012. http://4asstrategyfestival.com/storage/bronze_RPA_honda%20CR-V.pdf

Horovitz, B. October 31, 2013a. "GoDaddy Isn't Bringing Sexy Back to Super Bowl." *USA Today*, http://www.usatoday.com/story/money/business/2013/10/30/go-daddy-super-bowl-advertising-sexy-ads-danica-patrick/3308133/

Horovitz, B. December 13, 2013b. "$4M For Super Bowl Ad? Guess Who's Buying." *USA Today*, http://www.usatoday.com/story/money/business/2013/12/04/super-bowl-advertising-marketing-fox-commercials/3862761/

Howard, D.J.; and R.A. Kerin. 2004. "The Effects of Personalized Product Recommendations on Advertising Response Rates: The 'Try This. It Works!' Technique." *Journal of Consumer Psychology* 14, no. 3, pp. 271–79.

Huffman, C.; and B.E. Kahn. Autumn 1998. "Variety For Sale: Mass Customization or Mass Confusion?" *Journal of Retailing* 74, no. 4, pp. 491–513.

Jai, T.C.; L.D. Burns; and N.J. King. May 2013. "The Effect of Behavioral Tracking Practices on Consumers' Shopping Evaluations and Repurchase Intention Toward Trusted Online Retailers." *Computers in Human Behavior* 29, no. 3, pp. 901–9.

Kalyanaraman, S.; and S.S. Sundar. March 2006. "The Psychological Appeal of Personalized Content in Web Portals: Does Customization Affect Attitudes and Behavior?" *Journal of Communication* 56, no. 1, pp. 110–32.

Kiley, D. May 15, 2005. *A New Kind of Car Chase*, http://www.businessweek.com/stories/2005-05-15/a-new-kind-of-car-chase

Koller, D. December 5, 2011. "Death Knell For the Lecture: Technology as a Passport to Personalized Education." *New York Times*, http://www.nytimes.com/2011/12/06/science/daphne-koller-technology-as-a-passport-to-personalized-education.html?pagewanted=all

Kramer, T.; S. Spolter-Weisfeld; and M. Thakkar. March 2007. "The Effect of Cultural Orientation on Consumer Response to Personalization." *Marketing Science* 26, no.2, pp. 246–58.

Kreuter, M.W.; and C.S. Skinner. February 2000. "Tailoring: What's in a Name?" *Health Education Research* 15, no. 1, pp. 1–4.

Krishna, A.; and R. Ahluwalia. December 2008. "Language Choice in Advertising to Bilinguals: Asymmetric Effects for Multinationals Versus Local Firms." *Journal of Consumer Research* 35, no. 4, pp. 692–705.

Lampel, J.; and H. Mintzberg. Fall 1996. "Customizing Customization." *Sloan Management Review* 38, no. 1, pp. 21–30.

Lasswell, H.D. 1948. "The Structure and Function of Communication in Society." In *The Communication of Ideas*, eds. L. Bryson, 37–51. New York, NY: Harper & Brothers.

Lavidge, R.J.; and G.A. Steiner. October 1961. "A Model For Predictive Measurements of Advertising Effectiveness." *Journal of Marketing* 25, no.6, pp. 59–62.

Lee, T.B. July 15, 2013. "Gangnam Style Turns One Year Old Today." *Washington Post*, http://www.washingtonpost.com/blogs/wonkblog/wp/2013/07/15/gangnam-style-turns-one-year-old-today/

Levin, I.P.; and G.J. Gaeth. December 1988. "How Consumers Are Affected by the Framing of Attribute Information Before and After Consuming the Product." *Journal of Consumer Research* 15, no. 3, pp. 374–78.

Levin, I.P.; S.L. Schneider; and G.J. Gaeth. November 1998. "All Frames Are Not Created Equal: A Typology and Critical Analysis of Framing Effects." *Organizational Behavior and Human Decision Processes* 76, no. 2, pp. 149–88.

Levitt, T. May–June 1983. "The Globalization of Markets." *Harvard Business Review* 61, no. 3, pp. 92–102.

LG: Before You Text, Give it a Ponder. 2010. http://www.jaychiatawards.com/documents/gallery2010/631_LGMobileBeforeYouTextGiveItAPonder.pdf

Li, C. 2010. January–February 2010. "Primacy Effect or Recency Effect? A Long-Term Memory Test of Super Bowl Commercials." *Journal of Consumer Behaviour* 9, no. 1, pp. 32–44.

Li, C. March 2014. "A Tale of Two Social Networking Sites: How the Use of Facebook and Renren Influences Chinese Consumers' Attitudes Toward Product Packages With Different Cultural Symbols." *Computers in Human Behavior* 32, pp. 162–70.

Li, C.; and S. Kalyanaraman. May–June 2012. "What if Website Editorial Content and Ads are in Two Different Languages? A Study of Bilingual Consumers' Online Information Processing." *Journal of Consumer Behaviour* 11, no.3, pp. 198–206.

Li, C.; W. Tsai; and G. Soruco. 2013. "Perceived 'Hispanicness' Versus 'Americanness': A Study of Brand Ethnicity With Hispanic Consumers." *International Journal of Advertising* 32, no. 3, pp. 443–65.

Li, C.; and X. Wang. July 2013. "The Power of eWOM: A Re-Examination of Online Student Evaluations of Their Professors." *Computers in Human Behavior* 29, no. 4, pp. 1350–57.

Li, S.; Y. Sun; and Y. Wang. August 2007. "50% Off or Buy One Get One Free? Frame Preference as a Function of Consumable Nature in Dairy Products." *Journal of Social Psychology* 147, no. 4, pp. 413–21.

Lin, C. 2002. "Segmenting Customer Brand Preference: Demographic or Psychographic." *Journal of Product and Brand Management* 11, no. 4, pp. 249–68.

Luna, D.; and L.A. Peracchio. June 2005. "Sociolinguistic Effects on Code-Switched Ads Targeting Bilingual Consumers." *Journal of Advertising* 34, no. 2, pp. 43–56.

Luvs: Second Time Moms & The Truth About Parenting. 2013. http://www.aaaa.org/communications/2013%20Jay%20Chiat%20Case%20Studies/bronze_Saatchi_Luvs.pdf

Luvs Commercial: Breastfeeding. 2012. http://www.youtube.com/watch?v=ZgmbJso-2-o

Maslowska, E.; B. van den Putte; and E.G. Smit. December 2011. "The Effectiveness of Personalized E-Mail Newsletters and the Role of Personal Characteristics." *Cyberpsychology, Behavior, and Social Networking* 14, no.12, pp. 765–70.

Mattioli, D. August 23, 2012. "On Orbitz, Mac Users Steered to Pricier Hotels." *Wall Street Journal*, http://online.wsj.com/news/articles/SB10001424052702304458604577488822667325882

Miceli, G.N.; F. Ricotta; and M. Costabile. Spring 2007. "Customizing Customization: A Conceptual Framework for Interactive Personalization." *Journal of Interactive Marketing* 21, no. 2, pp. 6–25.

Miller, C.C. April 12, 2011. "How Useful is Google's Personalized Search?" *New York Times,* http://gadgetwise.blogs.nytimes.com/2011/04/12/how-useful-is-googles-personalized-search/

Miller, C.C. July 29, 2013. "Apps That Know What You Want, Before You Do." *New York Times,* http://www.nytimes.com/2013/07/30/technology/apps-that-know-what-you-want-before-you-do.html?pagewanted=all

Montgomery, A.L.; and M.D. Smith. May 2009. "Prospects For Personalization on the Internet." *Journal of Interactive Marketing* 23, no. 2, pp. 130–37.

Moon, Y. 2002. "Personalization and Personality: Some Effects of Customizing Message Style Based on Consumer Personality." *Journal of Consumer Psychology* 12, no. 4, pp. 313–26.

Moore, D.J.; W.D. Harris; and H.C. Chen. September 1995. "Affect Intensity: An Individual Difference Response to Advertising Appeals." *Journal of Consumer Research* 22, no. 2, pp. 154–64.

Moriarty, S.; N. Mitchell; and W. Wells. 2012. *Advertising & IMC: Principles and Practice.* 9th ed. Upper Saddle Rivers, NJ: Prentice Hall.

Morrison, M.A.; and E. Haley. June 2003. "Account Planners Views on How Their Work Is and Should Be Evaluated." *Journal of Advertising* 32, no. 2, pp. 7–16.

MRI+ Database. n.d. *Welcome to MRI+.* http://www.mriplus.com/site/index.aspx?AspxAutoDetectCookieSupport=1

Muniz, A.M.; and T.C. O' Guinn. March 2001. "Brand community." *Journal of Consumer Research* 27, no. 4, pp. 412–32.

Murray, K.B.; and G. Häubl. May 2009. "Personalization Without Interrogation: Towards More Effective Interactions Between Consumers and Feature-Based Recommendation Agents." *Journal of Interactive Marketing* 23, no. 2, pp. 138–46.

Newman, A.A. October 17, 2010. "Find Jay-Z's Memoir at a Bookstore, or on a Billboard." *New York Times,* http://www.nytimes.com/2010/10/18/business/media/18adco.html

Nielson. February 5, 2013. *Super Bowl XLVII Draws 108.7 Million Viewers, 26.1 Million Tweets*, http://www.nielsen.com/us/en/newswire/2013/super-bowl-xlvii-draws-108-7-million-viewers-26-1-tweets.html

Nike: NikeiD iPhone App. 2010. http://www.jaychiatawards.com/documents/gallery2010/768_NIKEiD.pdf

Nisbett, R.E.; and T.D. Wilson. May 1977. "Telling More Than We Can Know: Verbal Reports on Mental Processes." *Psychological Review* 84, no. 3, pp. 231–59.

Noar, S.M.; C.N. Benac; and M.S. Harris. July 2007. "Does Tailoring Matter? Meta-Analytic Review of Tailored Print Health Behavior Change Interventions." *Psychological Bulletin* 133, no. 4, pp. 673–93.

Noar, S.M.; N.G. Harrington; and R.S. Aldrich. 2009. "The Role of Message Tailoring in the Development of Persuasive Health Communication Messages." In *Communication Yearbook* (Vol.33), eds. C.S. Beck, 73–133. New York, NY: Routledge.

Nudd, T. January 9, 2013. "Gangnam Style's Psy to Star in Super Bowl Ad For Wonderful Pistachios." *Adweek*, http://www.adweek.com/news/advertising-branding/gangnam-styles-psy-star-super-bowl-ad-wonderful-pistachios-146392

Nuttin, J.M. September 1985. "Narcissism Beyond Gestalt and Awareness: The Name Letter Effect." *European Journal of Social Psychology* 15, no. 3, pp. 353–61.

O'Guinn, T.C.; R.J. Faber; and T.P. Meyer. September 1985. "Ethnic Segmentation and Spanish-Language Television." *Journal of Advertising* 14, no. 3, pp. 63–66.

Okazaki, S.; C.R. Taylor; and S. Zou. Fall 2006. "Advertising Standardization's Positive Impact on the Bottom Line: A Model of When and How Standardization Improves Financial and Strategic Performance." *Journal of Advertising* 35, no. 3, pp. 17–33.

Pampers: Pancitas in Concert. 2013. http://www.aaaa.org/communications/2013%20Jay%20Chiat%20Case%20Studies/HM_Conill_PAMPERS_BELLIES%20IN%20CONCERT.pdf

Pandora. January 15, 2014. *Pandora Launches Personalized Station Recommendations on iOS and Android Mobile Platforms*, http://online.wsj.com/article/PR-CO-20140115-906192.html

Patwardhan, P.; H. Patwardhan; and F. Vasavada-Oza. June 2011. "Does Planning Make Perfect? How Advertising Practitioners in India Perceive Account Planning." *Asian Journal of Communication* 21, no. 3, pp. 262–78.

Peppers, D.; M. Rogers; and B. Dorf. January–February 1999. "Is Your Company Ready For One-to-One Marketing?" *Harvard Business Review* 77, no. 1, pp. 151–60.

Petty, R.E.; and J.T. Cacioppo. 1986. *Communication and Persuasion: Central and Peripheral Routes to Attitude Change*. New York, NY: Springer-Verlag.

Petty, R.E.; S.C. Wheeler; and G.Y. Bizer. 2000. "Attitude Functions and Persuasion: An Elaboration Likelihood Approach to Matched Versus Mismatched Messages." In *Why We Evaluate: Functions of Attitudes*, eds. G.R. Maio; and J.M. Olson, 133–62. Mahwah, NJ: Erlbaum.

Pilling, V.K.; and L.A. Brannon. 2007. "Assessing College Students' Attitudes Toward Responsible Drinking Messages to Identify Promising Binge Drinking Intervention Strategies." *Health Communication* 22, no. 3, pp. 265–76.

Porter, S.R.; and M.E. Whitcomb. 2003. "The Impact of Contact Type on Web Survey Response Rates." *Public Opinion Quarterly* 67, no. 4, pp. 579–88.

Postma, O.J.; and M. Brokke. January 2002. "Personalisation in Practice: The Proven Effects of Personalisation." *Journal of Database Marketing* 9, no. 2, pp. 137–42.

Potter, W.J.; E. Forrest; B.S. Sapolsky; and W. Ware. April–May 1988. "Segmenting VCR owners." *Journal of Advertising Research* 28, no. 2, pp. 29–39.

Putrevu, S. June 2008. "Consumer Responses Toward Sexual and Nonsexual Appeals: The Influence of Involvement, Need For Cognition (NFC), and Gender." *Journal of Advertising* 37, no. 2, pp. 57–69.

Raman, N.V.; P. Chattopadhyay; and W.D. Hoyer. 1995. "Do Consumers Seek Emotional Situations: The Need For Emotion Scale." In *Advances in Consumer Research* (Vol. 22), eds. F.R. Kardes; and M. Sujan, 537–42. Provo, UT : Association for Consumer Research.

Rattray, B. November 4, 2011. "Victory Over Debit Fee is a Sign of Consumer Power." *CNN*. http://www.cnn.com/2011/11/04/opinion/rattray-consumers-fight-back/

Reichert, T. December 2002. "Sex in Advertising Research: A Review of Content, Effects, and Functions of Sexual Information in Consumer Advertising." *Annual Review of Sex Research* 13, no. 1, pp. 241–73.

Reichert, T.; and C. Carpenter. December 2004. "An Update on Sex in Magazine Advertising: 1983 to 2003." *Journalism and Mass Communication Quarterly* 81, no. 4, pp. 823–37.

Reichert, T.; J. Lambiase; S. Morgan; M. Carstarphen; and S. Zavoina. March 1999. "Cheesecake and Beefcake: No Matter How You Slice it, Sexual Explicitness in Advertising Continues to Increase." *Journalism and Mass Communication Quarterly* 76, no. 1, pp. 7–20.

Richards, J.I.; and C.M. Curran. Summer 2002. "Oracles on 'Advertising': Searching For a Definition." *Journal of Advertising* 31, no. 2, pp. 63–77.

Rogers, E. 1962. *Diffusion of Innovations*. New York, NY: Free Press.

Roslow, P.; and J.A.F. Nicholls. May–June 1996. "Targeting the Hispanic Market: Comparative Persuasion of TV Commercials in Spanish and English." *Journal of Advertising Research* 36, no. 3, pp. 67–77.

Ruiz, S.; and M. Sicilia. June 2004. "The Impact of Cognitive and/or Affective Processing Styles on Consumer Response to Advertising Appeals." *Journal of Business Research* 57, no. 6, pp. 657–64.

Sasser, S.L.; and S. Koslow. December 2008. "Desperately Seeking Advertising Creativity." *Journal of Advertising* 37, no. 4, pp. 5–19.

Snyder, C.R. March 1992. "Product Scarcity by Need For Uniqueness Interaction: A Consumer Catch-22 Carousel?" *Basic and Applied Social Psychology* 13, no. 1, pp. 9–24.

Schmid, S.; and T. Kotulla. October 2011. "50 Years of Research on International Standardization and Adaptation—From a Systematic Literature Analysis to a Theoretical Framework." *International Business Review* 20, no. 5, pp. 491–507.

Schumann, D.W.; J.M. Hathcote; and S. West. September 1991. "Corporate Advertising in America: A Review of Published Studies on Use, Measurement, and Effectiveness." *Journal of Advertising* 20, no. 3, pp. 35–56.

Sharma, A. January 14, 2014. "Viacom to Launch Customized Kids' TV Channel." *Wall Street Journal,* http://online.wsj.com/news/articles/SB10001 424052702303754404579312904182126302

Shen, A.; and A.D. Ball. April 2009. "Is Personalization of Services Always a Good Thing? Exploring the Role of Technology-Mediated Personalization (TMP) in Service Relationships." *Journal of Services Marketing* 23, no. 2, pp. 79–91.

Simonson, I. January 2005. "Determinants of Customers' Responses to Customized Offers: Conceptual Framework and Research Propositions." *Journal of Marketing* 69, no. 1, pp. 32–45.

Singelis, T.M. October 1994. "The Measurement of Independent and Interdependent Self-Construals." *Personality and Social Psychology Bulletin* 20, no. 5, pp. 580–91.

Singer, N. January 4, 2014. "Listen to Pandora, and It Listens Back." *New York Times,* http://www.nytimes.com/2014/01/05/technology/pandora-mines-users-data-to-better-target-ads.html

Smith. H.J., T. Dinev; and H. Xu. December 2011. "Information Privacy Research: An Interdisciplinary Review." *MIS Quarterly* 35, no. 4, pp. 989–1015.

Smith, H.J.; S.J. Milberg; and S.J. Burke. June 1996. "Information Privacy: Measuring Individuals' Concerns About Organizational Practices." *MIS Quarterly* 20, no. 2, pp. 167–96.

Smith, R.E., J. Chen; and X. Yang. Winter 2008. "The Impact of Advertising Creativity on the Hierarchy of Effects." *Journal of Advertising* 37, no. 4, pp. 47–61.

Smith, R.E.; and X. Yang. June 2004. "Toward a General Theory of Creativity in Advertising: Examining the Role of Divergence." *Marketing Theory* 4, no. 1–2, pp. 31–58.

Smith, W.R. July 1956. "Product Differentiation and Market Segmentation as Alternative Marketing Strategies." *Journal of Marketing* 21, no. 1, pp. 3–8.

Snyder, C.R.; and H.L. Fromkin. October 1977. "Abnormality as a Positive Characteristic: The Development and Validation of a Scale Measuring Need For Uniqueness." *Journal of Abnormal Psychology* 86, no. 5, pp. 518–27.

Spector, M.; and J.A. Trachtenberg. July 20, 2011. "Borders Succumbs to Digital Era in Books." *Wall Street Journal*, http://online.wsj.com/news/articles/SB10 001424052702304567604576456430727129532

Spotts, H.E.; M.G. Weinberger; and A.L. Parsons. September 1997. "Assessing the Use and Impact of Humor on Advertising Effectiveness: A Contingency Approach." *Journal of Advertising* 26, no. 3, pp. 17–32.

Stein, J. March 10, 2011. "Data Mining: How Companies Now Know Everything About You." *Time*, http://content.time.com/time/magazine/article/0,9171,2058205-1,00.html

Stewart, D.D.; C.B. Stewart; C. Tyson; G. Vinci; and T. Fioti. August 2004. "Serial Position Effects and the Picture-Superiority Effect in the Group Recall of Unshared Information." *Group Dynamics: Theory, Research, and Practice* 8, no. 3, pp. 166–81.

Stone, G.; D. Besser; and L.E. Lewis. 2000. "Recall, Liking, and Creativity in TV Commercials: A New Approach." *Journal of Advertising Research* 40, no. 3, pp. 7–18.

Strategic Business Insights. n.d. *The US VALS™ Survey*, http://www.strategicbusinessinsights.com/vals/presurvey.shtml

Strategic Business Insights. n.d. *US Framework and VALS™ Types*, http://www.strategicbusinessinsights.com/vals/ustypes.shtml

Sundar, S.S. 2004. "Loyalty to Computer Terminals: Is It Anthropomorphism or Consistency?" *Behaviour and Information Technology* 23, no. 2, pp. 107–18.

Sundar, S.S.; and S.S. Marathe. July 2010. "Personalization Versus Customization: The Importance of Agency, Privacy, and Power Usage." *Human Communication Research* 36, no. 3, pp. 298–322.

Syam, N.; P. Krishnamurthy; and J.D. Hess. May–June 2008. "That's What I Thought I Wanted? Miswanting and Regret For a Standard Good in a Mass-Customized World." *Marketing Science* 27, no. 3, pp. 379–97.

Tam, K.Y.; S.Y. Ho. December 2006. "Understanding the Impact of Web Personalization on User Information Processing and Decision Outcomes." *MIS Quarterly* 30, no. 4, pp. 865–90.

Taylor, T.D. December 2009. "Advertising and the Conquest of Culture." *Social Semiotics* 19, no. 4, pp. 405–25.

Tian, K.T.; W.O. Bearden; G.L. Hunter. June 2001. "Consumers' Need For Uniqueness: Scale Development and Validation." *Journal of Consumer Research* 28, no. 1, pp. 50–66.

Triandis, H.C. 1995. *Individualism and Collectivism*. Boulder, CO: Westview.

Tsai, W.S.; and C. Li. May 2012. "Bicultural Advertising and Hispanic Acculturation." *Hispanic Journal of Behavioral Sciences* 34, no. 2, pp. 305–22.

Tversky, A.; and D. Kahneman. September 1973. "Availability: A Heuristic For Judging Frequency and Probability." *Cognitive Psychology* 5, no. 2, pp. 207–32.

Tversky, A.; and D. Kahneman. January 1981. "The Framing of Decisions and the Psychology of Choice." *Science* 211, no. 4481, pp. 453–58.

United Breaks Guitars. 2009. http://www.youtube.com/watch?v=5YGc4zOqozo

Van Doorn, J.; and J.C. Hoekstra. December 2013. "Customization of Online Advertising: The Role of Intrusiveness." *Marketing Letters* 24, no. 4, pp. 339–51.

Vakratsas, D.; and T. Ambler. January 1999. "How Advertising Works: What Do We Really Know?" *Journal of Marketing* 63, no. 1, pp. 26–43.

Vesanen, J.; and M. Raulas. Winter 2006. "Building Bridges For Personalization: A Process Model For Marketing." *Journal of Interactive Marketing* 20, no. 1, pp. 5–20.

Weilbacher, W.M. November–December 2001. "Point of View: Does Advertising Cause a 'Hierarchy of Effects'?" *Journal of Advertising Research* 41, no. 6, pp. 19–26.

Weinberger, M.G.; and C.S. Gulas. December 1992. "The Impact of Humor in Advertising: A Review." *Journal of Advertising* 21, no. 4, pp. 35–59.

Weinberger, M.G.; H.E. Spotts; L. Campbell; and A.L. Parsons. May–June 1995. "The Use and Effect of Humor in Different Advertising Media." *Journal of Advertising Research* 35, no. 3, pp. 44–56.

West, D.C.; A.J. Kover; and A. Caruana. 2008. "Practitioner and Customer Views of Advertising Creativity." *Journal of Advertising* 37, no. 4, pp. 35–45.

White, T.B.; D.L. Zahay; H. Thorbjørnsen; and S. Shavitt. March 2008. "Getting Too Personal: Reactance to Highly Personalized Email Solicitation." *Marketing Letters* 19, no. 1, pp. 39–50.

Wind, J.; and A. Rangaswamy. Winter 2001. "Customerization: The Next Revolution in Mass Customization." *Journal of Interactive Marketing* 15, no. 1, pp. 13–32.

Wogalter, M.S.; B.M. Racicot; M.J. Kalsher; and S.N. Simpson. October 1994. "Personalization of Warning Signs: The Role of Perceived Relevance on Behavioral Compliance." *International Journal of Industrial Ergonomics* 14, no. 3, pp. 233–42.

World's Most Admired Companies. n.d. http://money.cnn.com/magazines/fortune/most-admired/

Xie, E.; H. Teo; and W. Wan. January 2006. "Volunteering Personal Information on the Internet: Effects of Reputation, Privacy Notices, and Rewards on Online Consumer Behavior." *Marketing Letters* 17, no. 1, pp. 61–74.

Yoo, C.; and D. MacInnis. October 2005. "The Brand Attitude Formation Process of Emotional and Informational Ads." *Journal of Business Research* 58, no. 10, pp. 1397–406.

Index

Account planning, 6
Advertising
    attitude, 14–15
    behavior, 15–16
    creativity in, 7–9
    entertraining, 10–12
    informative, 9–12
    memory, 12–14
    new meanings of, 3–5
    strategy in, 5–7
    traditional definition, 1–2
Attitude, 14–15
Attribute framing, 83

Back translation, 69
Behavior, 15–16
Behavioral segmentation, 45
Business value proposition
    individualized strategy, 55–57
    standardized strategy, 31–33
    targeted strategy, 43–46

Collectivistic tendency, 60
Consumer insights
    content matching, 79–82
    delivering information, 84–86
    do's and don'ts, 86–89
    framing effects, 82–84
    individualized strategy, 61–62
    standardized strategy, 34–37
    targeted strategy, 48–50
Consumers' expectation
    individualized strategy, 58–61
    standardized strategy, 33–34
    targeted strategy, 47–48
Consumers preferences
    customization, 72–73
    do's and don'ts, 74–77
    long-term knowledge, 70–72
    personalization, 73
    predicting, 72–74
    short-term knowledge, 67–70

standardized strategy, 21–23
Content matching, 79–82
Conventional mass media, 3
Corporate advertising, 39
Corporate social responsibility, 39–40
Crafting messages
    individualized strategy, 63–65
    standardized strategy, 37–38
    targeted strategy, 50–53
Creative brief, 6–7
Creativity in advertising, 7–9
Customization, 72–73

Diffusion of innovations, 45–46

Elaboration Likelihood Model
    (ELM), 10
ELM. *See* Elaboration Likelihood
    Model
Emotional approach, advertising,
    10–12
Essence magazine, 25
Ethnographic observation, 68

Facebook, 59
Framing effects, 82–84

Glamour magazine, 25
Goal framing, 83
Goodwill advertising, 39

Harvard Business Review, 22

Individualized advertising
    advantages of, 94–95
    communication, 28–29
    consumer insights, 61–62
    consumers' expectation, 58–61
    crafting messages, 63–65
    drawbacks of, 95

explanation of, 26–27
idea/goal of, 26
integrating of, 96–99
proposition, business value, 55–57
Individualized communication, 28–29
Informational advertising, 9–12
Institutional advertising, 39
Interpersonal media, 3

Journal of Advertising, 1
Journal of Communication, 82
Journal of Consumer Research, 80
Journal of Marketing, 12

Levitt, Theodore, 22
Long-term knowledge, consumers
    preferences, 70–72

Market segmentation, 23–24
Mass media, 3
Memory, 12–14

Need for uniqueness, 60
New York Times, 76

Personalization, 73
Personalized search, 60
Predictive search, 57
Primacy effects, 86
Privacy paradox, 76
Psychographic segmentation, 44
Psychology reactance, 75

Qualitative research, 67–69
Quantitative research, 68

Rational approach, advertising, 10–12
Recency effects, 86
Risk choice framing, 83

Serial position effects, 86
Sexual content, 38–39

Short-term knowledge, consumers
    preferences, 67–70
Social media, 4
Standardized advertising
    advantages of, 92
    benefits, 20
    campaigns, 39–40
    consumer insights, 34–37
    consumers' expectation, 33–34
    consumers preferences, 21–23
    corporate social responsibility,
        39–40
    crafting messages, 37–38
    description of, 19–20
    drawbacks of, 92–93
    importance of, 24–26
    integrating of, 96–99
    promoting, 21
    proposition, business value, 31–33
    sexual appeals, 38–39
Strategy
    account planning, 6
    creative brief, 6–7
    individualized (*See* Individualized
        advertising)
    standardized (*See* Standardized
        advertising)
    targeted (*See* Targeted advertising)

Targeted advertising
    advantages of, 93
    campaigns, 39–40
    consumer insights, 48–50
    consumers' expectation, 47–48
    crafting messages, 50–53
    drawbacks of, 93–94
    idea/logic of, 23
    importance of, 24–26
    integrating of, 96–99
    market segmentation, 23–24
    proposition, business value, 43–46
Time magazine, 75

Wall Street Journal, 27

www.ingramcontent.com/pod-product-compliance
Lightning Source LLC
Chambersburg PA
CBHW062034200326
41519CB00017B/5036